W9-CJJ-375

HOCKEY'S
Book of
FIRSTS

HOCKEY'S
Book of
FIRSTS

by James Duplacey

JG
PRESS

Published by World Publications Group, Inc.
140 Laurel Street
East Bridgewater, MA 02333
www.wrldpub.net

ISBN 1-57215-037-8
978-1-57215-037-9

Printed and bound in China by SNP Leefung Printers Limited

1 2 3 4 5   06 05 03 02

PAGE 2: Vector hockey sticks, oversized equipment, helmets
and visors, Aeroflex goalie pads and moldable skates are all new
innovations to ice hockey.

THIS PAGE: Whether you call it the twine tent, the corded
cottage or the hempen hut — it's still just a hockey net.

DEDICATION: This book is dedicated to my mother, Dorothy
Mary (Currie) Duplacey 1919-2001.

The publishers would like to thank Joe Lynch and Lloyd Johnson
for their assistance.

CONTENTS

FOREWORD

The game of ice hockey has an unusual and varied past that continues to spur debate among historians of the game. Unlike many of its professional contemporaries, such as baseball and basketball, the exact time and place of the sport's origin has never been firmly established. Three different locations — Montreal, Kingston and Nova Scotia — have all claimed ownership of the game's birthright, and spokespeople for each of these regions will defend their position with the calculated vigor of a crafty chess player. They will also argue vehemently and aggressively for the honor of claiming their district as the official no-doubt-about-it-hands-down "Home of Hockey." If you've ever attended a Society of International Hockey Research (SIHR) convention and this topic is thrown on the floor for discussion, you'll instantly discover that the roaring rhetoric that accompanies such a debate is often more enjoyable than the on-ice product these word-wise warriors are attempting to defend.

Throughout its 130-year history, ice hockey has also suffered from a "weak paper trail." In the early years, detailed newspaper accounts were sporadic, confusing and controversial, and accurate game sheets were poorly filed, waylaid or lost. While the history of baseball has always been meticulously detailed — thanks in large part to the leisurely pace of the game and the simplistic beauty of the box score — hockey has not been so lucky. Not only are some of the early facts and facets of the game still in doubt, there are still historical questions concerning games and players who competed in the National Hockey League. Each year, some keen-eyed hockey historian will draft a letter to the NHL offices claiming he has discovered a new player, a lost statistic or a revised rule that somehow escaped through the cracks of time in the ice palaces of history. And upon further review, more often than not, this finding is proven to be correct. Even as I write this, I just received a well-documented and detailed argument from a fan who claims a gentleman named Clement Piche played for the Montreal Canadiens during the 1921–22 season. The jury's still out on that one. I'll get back to you.

There are other factors that have made the sport we love both a researcher's migraine nightmare and a bountiful treasure trove. Unlike most other professional sports, hockey has a worldwide playing field and it is painted on a universal canvas. Hockey has as rich and confusing a history in Europe as it has in North America. And although the basic rules of the game are the same, there are vital differences in the way the game is played and the way the rules are deciphered in North America and Europe. In the search for noteworthy firsts, this aspect of hockey's global appeal opened up a whole new net full of problematic pucks.

And so, this is the inconclusive inkwell that I stuck my pen into when I started my research for this book. Since we couldn't dedicate as much time and space to the evolution of the European game, we concentrated on North American hockey firsts. However, there is an exhaustive section on European firsts in the

TOP: Colin Kilburn (left) listens intently to the instructions of coach Dick Irvin.
ABOVE: On March 1, 1988, Wayne Gretzky became the NHL's all-time leading set-up artist when he registered assist #1050, surpassing his idol, Gordie Howe.
BELOW: Coach is Cornered — Don Cherry, whose flamboyant orations on the game of hockey have made him a cultural icon in Canada, gives the "thumbs-up" to a group of NHL prospects.

North American game, including the names of the first European players from over 20 different countries to be drafted by NHL franchises. I thank my good friend and fellow hockey historian Patrick Houda for helping complete the legwork on this particular section of what I feel is a wonderfully diverse chapter in hockey history.

I attempted to steer clear of the obvious firsts that could be found on the pages of any record book. Instead, I tried to peer into the wild and wooly wasteland of ice hockey history. This book delves into the evolution of hockey, from the equipment to the rules to the ice it is played on. It offers praise to the architects who helped build the foundation of the game and the graceful athletes who helped hockey grow from a sport that once had two pro leagues and seven teams to one that is played worldwide.

Hockey's Book of Firsts is divided into a number of categories that has left no aspect of the game ignored. From the players themselves to the coaches, referees, owners and scribes, their stories are included inside these covers. From the grand old barns in which the world's fastest game has been played to the rules, the tools and the fools, the facts and the frictions, we have covered every aspect of the sport like a bad Bobby Hull toupee. In fact, if you want to know how many former players claim that they were responsible for thieving Bobby Hull's hairpiece on that dramatic WHA evening, this is the place to look.

If it's brains and not brawn that stokes your hockey flames, this is where you can read about the smartest team in hockey history, a squad that once included a former Nuremberg trial lawyer, a future NHL president, a future Canadian Prime Minister and a future Canadian Governor-General. This book of firsts is probably the only tome where the peerless pursuer of pure hockey pabulum can find the first player to wear a three digit number on his sweater and also discover the names of those players whose off-ice claims to fame overshadowed their performance in the rink.

In selecting the categories, I attempted to find as many instances as I could where some timeworn and oft-asked questions — such as the first goalie to wear a mask or the first defenseman to record 100 points in a season — have delightfully new and surprising answers.

There are plenty of other tidbits, anecdotes and headlines scattered throughout the book. And like the game itself, *Hockey's Book of Firsts* has a few questionable calls that leaves plenty of ice time for lively debate among the dedicated denizens of the on-ice drama we call hockey.

I have tried to make this book as amusing as it is enlightening. I trust I have achieved a little of both. So settle into a sin-bin of your choice, tie down your jersey, loosen up your skates, open up a pop and enjoy.

James Duplacey

ABOVE: Dick Irvin, pictured here as a member of the WCHL's Portland Rosebuds, was a Hall of Fame player before becoming one of the most respected and revered coaches in NHL history. **BELOW**: In 1907-08, Grindy Forrester was a member of the Winnipeg Maple Leafs, one of four teams that comprised the Manitoba Professional Hockey League, the first pro loop formed in Canada.

THE PLAYERS

T his section relates to those proud purveyors of the pond, the players who made the game the flashy sport it has become. From the dashing defensemen to the power forwards and those lovable custodians of the corded crease, their accomplishments, awards, foibles and, yes, failures can be found here.

Hockey is a constantly evolving sport, realigning and reinventing itself in order to adjust to a generation of players who are larger and faster than their ancestors. And, in the past decade, the game has opened its doors to women, and their contributions are noted in detail.

Today's game is faster and more physical than ever. The players in this era of the game, at almost every level, are fine honed machines and physical marvels who can skate, shoot and hit with ferocious ability. The modern goaltenders are human pretzels who can bend like a Slinky and move like a panther. When Phil Esposito (6'1", 205 lbs.) was the dominant offensive player in the NHL, he was also among the largest players in the league. Espo put himself in the Hockey Hall of Fame by planting himself squarely in the slot in front of the net. Today, the bluelines of the NHL are patrolled by hulking goliaths like Zdeno Chara (6'11"), Matt Johnson (6'7"), Sami Helenius (6'6"), Chris Pronger (6'6"), Mike Wilson (6'6") and Chris McAllister (6'8"). With bruisers like that lurking around, it's hard to imagine that a forward of Espo's stature could withstand the punishment he would be subjected to in this era of the league.

So, it's important for us to acknowledge the achievements of those players who played the game when it was a finesse sport where skill and not size was the measure used to gauge a player's ability. Many of those names, like Herb Foster, Gerry Glaude and Hippo Galloway, can be found here.

Since the recorded history of hockey has numerous gray areas because of lost or misplaced files and sloppy housekeeping, the role of the hockey historian has become essential in reestablishing the paper trail of the game's past. Organizations such as the Society for International Hockey Research (SIHR) and the Hockey Research Association (HRA) have played impressive and important roles in putting hockey's historical house in order. Dedicated researchers such as John Paton, Ernie Fitzsimmons, Patrick Houda, Bill Fitsell, Robert Duff and James Karkowski have been instrumental in finding lost players, unearthing forgotten facts and settling statistical debates.

As you peruse this section, raise a glass to them and enjoy the game.

OPPOSITE: Steve Rucchin of the Anaheim Mighty Ducks is one of the few players drafted out of the Canadian College system to go to the NHL.
BELOW: Before the installation of Plexiglas above the boards in the late 1940s, patrons attending games at Maple Leafs Gardens were protected by panels of wire meshing. That's Bashin' Bill Barilko of the Leafs giving a young Red Wing protégé his first NHL "screen" test.

Goaltenders

First goalie to score a goal
Hey, Ma, That's Me Up on the Scoreboard!

1971
1979

ABOVE: Charlie Rayner was renowned for his dashes up the ice attempting to become the first netminder to score a goal in a NHL game.
ABOVE RIGHT: Even Michel Plasse (pictured here with Colorado) must have applauded Lexington Man O' War goaltender Mike Smith. Smith was the first goalie to score a goal, post a shutout and record his first professional victory in the same game.
RIGHT: San Jose Sharks' Evgeni Nabokov joined an elite group of goaltender goal-scorers when he drifted a shot into the vacated Vancouver net on March 10, 2002.

The first professional netminder to score a goal was Michel Plasse of the Central Hockey League's Kansas City Blues. In a game against Oklahoma City on February 21, 1971, Plasse intercepted an errant pass and lofted the puck down the ice into the opposing goal to cement a 3-1 K.C. victory.

The first NHL twine-tender to be credited with scoring a goal was Battlin' Billy Smith of the NY Islanders. During a game against the Colorado Rockies on November 28, 1979, the Isles were assessed a delayed penalty. As an extra Colorado attacker was hurrying to join the attack, Colorado defender Rob Ramage stepped over the blueline and ripped a shot towards the Islanders' cage. After Smith casually deflected the shot into the corner, Ramage roared into the Islanders' zone, secured possession of the rebound and feathered a pass back to the point. Unfortunately, Ramage forgot that he was the player who was supposed to be manning that position and the puck rolled down the ice into the Rockies' net. The last Islanders player to touch the puck was Billy Smith and he was awarded credit for scoring the goal.

In terms of actually shooting and scoring, Philadelphia's Ron Hextall can claim that he was the first NHL goalie to actually deposit a puck into an opposing net when his chip shot from 60 yards bounced and rolled directly into the Boston Bruins' cup on December 8, 1987. Not long after that, Hextall became the first NHL twine-tender to score a goal in the post-season, when he drifted a shot over into the vacated Washington Capitals cage on April 11, 1989.

But first is first, and the first was also second. That double honor belongs to Fred Brophy of the Montreal Westmounts. In a game against Quebec, Brophy snuck down the ice and became the first netminder to score a goal when he slipped a shot past Paddy Moran on February 18, 1905. The following season, Brophy duplicated his feat by scoring against Victorias' cage keeper Nathan Frye on March 7, 1906.

The first goalie to use a "trapper"

The Old "Block and Trapper" Routine, Eh?

1947

From the earliest days of the sport, goaltenders wore gloves that were almost identical to the mitts modeled by forwards and defensemen. Chicago's Emile "The Cat" Francis changed goaltending fashion forever when he wore a specially designed first baseman's mitt with an extended protective wrapping on the wrist during a 1947–48 tilt with the Detroit Red Wings.

Detroit bench boss Jack Adams immediately protested that Francis' new toy belonged on the diamond, not on the ice. NHL President Clarence Campbell gave the matter consideration and after some debate, approved Francis' innovation. And so, the "catcher" or "trapper" was born. Not content to be a one-handed innovator, Francis can also take credit for introducing the "blocker" to the goaltenders' arsenal, although some pundits insist he share honors with Boston crease cop Frankie Brimsek. Shortly after winning his "trapper" victory, the "Cat" taped an outer layer of sponge rubber to his stick-hand glove. This eventually evolved into what is now the modern blocker.

The first goalie
to use a water bottle
Cool, Clear Water

BELOW: When Edmonton Oilers' g.m. Glen Sather first observed a water bottle resting on top of the net, he quipped, "What are they going to want up there next, a bucket of chicken?"
BOTTOM: Bob Froese led the NHL in victories during the 1985-86 season.

For generations, goaltenders resembled the on-ice version of comic Rodney Dangerfield — they didn't get any respect. They were expected to play every minute of every game and if they got cut, they got stitched up and went back out to face another round of rubber. And if they dared ask permission to use a facemask, they were usually given a ticket to the bus leagues.

That was then, this is now. By the mid-1980s, goalies were modeling lightweight pads, full body armor, custom-fitted head-wear and gloves the size of butterfly nets. But there was still one thing the players had that the goalie didn't: access to water. Goalies had to wait until a stoppage in play to procure some liquid refreshment, while the other lugs who were making the big bucks could belly up to the trough anytime they liked. That all changed on March 16, 1985. During the NCAA Champion-ship tournament, Providence College goaltender Chris Terreri and Boston University twine-tender Scott Gordon both skated to their respective cages and placed a plastic water bottle on the top of the net. It was a brilliant act of goaltender solidarity. Since both goalies were using a water bottle, the playing field was balanced.

That wasn't the case when the now familiar plastic container made its first appearance in the NHL. During the playoff series between Philadelphia and the NY Islanders in 1985, Philly net-minder Bob Froese became the first NHL goalie to use a water bottle. This caused consternation, conflict and cat calls from the opposing team, who claimed the bottle would soon be flying, sliding and spilling all over the rink. But the referee calmly informed the Flyers' bitter rivals that since Froese was securing the bottle to the top of the net with a strip of Velcro, he was free to drink and drive. It was a refreshing idea that quickly became a staple in the goaltender's toolbox.

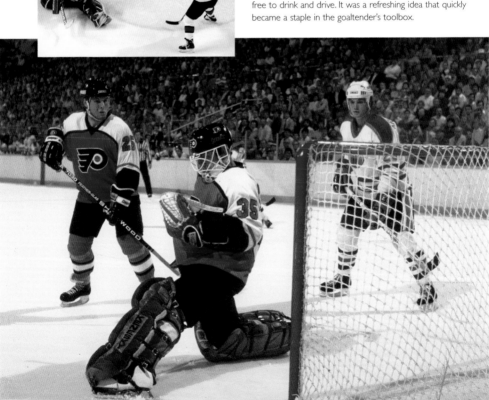

First goalie to be named captain of a team
Clipping the Roach

1923

When the NHL passed legislation that designated the captain of the hockey club as the only player who had permission to converse with the referee during a game, Toronto St. Pats' coach Eddie Powers decided to rest the rule by naming his goaltender as the team captain. Powers reasoned that if he needed to stall for time or give his club a break to regenerate their engines, he'd just have the goalie start a debate with the referee.

John Ross Roach was the netkeeper for the St. Pats at the time so, by default, he became the first goaltender to be named captain of a NHL team. Nicknamed "Little Napoleon" for his temper, size and attitude, he was probably not the wisest of choices. During the 1932–33 campaign, there were four goaltenders serving as captains — George Hainsworth, Roy Worters, Charlie Gardiner, and Alex Connell. When Gardiner backstopped his Chicago Black Hawks team all the way into the Stanley Cup winner's circle, he became the first — and only — goaltender to captain a Stanley Cup championship team.

It wasn't until the 1947–48 season that another goaltender was adorned with the captain's "C." Prior to the opening game on the schedule, Canadiens' coach Dick Irvin shocked the skeptics by naming Bill Durnan as team captain. Irvin's rationale was based on the same logic that Eddie Powers had used decades earlier and Durnan responded like a trooper by harping at the refs and yapping at the opposition.

To alleviate Durnan's persistent "yak" attacks, the NHL implemented Rule 14 (D), which prohibits goalies from serving as team captains.

The first goalie to register 100 career shutouts

By George, He's the Real Mr. Zero

1936

One NHL record that most scribes deem as being safe for all time is Terry "Uke" Sawchuk's mark of 103 career shutouts. As of this writing, no active goalie had even reached the 70-shutout mark so it's safe to assume that Sawchuk's milestone mark is secure.

While there's no doubt that Sawchuk was one of the greatest goaltenders ever to stand between the pipes, he does not hold the professional record for shutouts, nor was he the first netminder to reach the century mark in blanking the opposition. That honor rests in the capable mitts of George Hainsworth, the dandy puck stopper who was given the unenviable task of replacing the legendary Georges Vezina in the crease of the Montreal Canadiens after Vezina succumbed to tuberculosis in 1926. Hainsworth responded to the challenge by capturing the Vezina Trophy as the NHL's top goaltender in the first three years the trophy was presented.

The diminutive netminder blanked the opposition 104 times in major professional league (WCHL, WHL and NHL) competition. That's one more zero notched on his resume than Mr. Sawchuk recorded. Hainsworth became the first goalie to reach the century mark in shutouts during the 1935–36 season when he was a member of the Toronto Maple Leafs.

First goaltender to become a NHL coach
Crease Crazy

1921

BELOW: Odie Cleghorn (left), the coach of Pittsburgh's first NHL franchise, counts out boxing promoter and team owner Benny Leonard, who is hanging off the crossbar like a punch drunk boxer on the ropes.

BELOW RIGHT: Lester Patrick's sly coaching style earned him the nickname "The Silver Fox."

Hugh Lehman was the first NHL goaltender nutty enough to become a NHL coach. After facing rubber bullets 8 amateur and 17 professional seasons, Lehman obviously hadn't taken enough punishment, so he stepped behind the Chicago bench early in the 1927–28 NHL season and proved to himself and his boss that he was more adept at stopping pucks than preventing losses. His Black Hawks squad managed only 3 victories in the 21 games he was in charge of his charges and he was put out of his misery when the season ended.

However, you could make a case that Pittsburgh Pirates' player-coach Odie Cleghorn was the first goalie to be a coach. Cleghorn was forced to don the pads on February 23, 1926, when Roy "Shrimp" Worters was unable to take his position between the pipes for a match against the powerhouse Montreal Canadiens. Cleghorn proved to be a more-than-able understudy, backstopping the Buccaneers to a 3-2 victory over the Habs.

But the first goalie to become a coach was actually a coach who was a player who became a goalie. During the 1921–22 season, Lester Patrick was doing double duty as the playing coach of the PCHA's Vancouver Aristocrats. During that season, Patrick volunteered to spend ten harrowing minutes between the pipes when incumbent goaltender Hec Fowler was forced from the game after taking a puck in the kisser.

Patrick was hardly stellar, allowing one goal in his ten-minute stay in the cage, but it was a worthy dress rehearsal for his greatest moment in the NHL spotlight. During the 1928 Stanley Cup finals, the Silver Fox — now the coach of the NHL's NY Rangers — was forced to replace injured Lorne Chabot in goal. Patrick rose to the occasion, stopping 17 of 18 shots in helping the Broadway Blueshirts escape with a 2-1 overtime victory over the Montreal Maroons. Old Les was also the first man to coach two Stanley Cup-winning teams in two different leagues, guiding the WCHL's Victoria Cougars to the top of the Stanley Cup ladder in 1925 before doing the same with the NY Rangers in 1928 and 1933.

First goalie to lose a game without giving up a goal
Cooked Goose

1989

BELOW: Mario Gosselin was dubbed "Goose" by Team Canada coach Dave King during the 1988 Winter Olympics.

Mario Gosselin probably would have chosen an easier way to put his name in the NHL history books. When LA Kings cage plumber Kelly Hrudey was injured in the third period of a Los Angeles-Edmonton game in 1989, Gosselin took over for his wounded teammate. At the time, the Kings were losing to the Oilers by a slim single-goal margin. In the final minute of the contest, Kings' coach Robbie Ftorek yanked the Goose for an extra attacker only to see the Oilers slide a puck into the empty net for a 7-5 lead. Moments after Gosselin returned to the Kings' cage, Los Angeles scored to pull within a goal, but the match ended before the Kings could nail the equalizer, going into the record books as a 7-6 Edmonton victory.

Since Gosselin was the goalie of record when the Oilers scored their 7th goal — which turned out to be the winning marker — the Goose goal was charged with the loss, even though he didn't allow a goal while he was in the Kings' crease.

First NHL goaltender to play 100 games without a shutout

Shutdown in Shutouts

1989

During his lengthy professional career, Eldon "Pokey" Reddick has stepped between the pipes wearing the uniform of 13 different teams in five different leagues. He has recorded 23 shutouts, shared the IHL's top goaltending award with teammate Rick St. Croix in 1986 and captured the IHL's most valuable playoff performer trophy when he compiled a perfect 12-0 post-season record in guiding the Fort Wayne Komets to the league championship.

In addition to these minor league accolades, Reddick also enjoyed a respectable NHL career, compiling a 46-58-16 record with Winnipeg, Edmonton and Florida. Along the way he carved a niche for himself in the NHL record book, although it's doubtful he enjoyed the journey.

On January 13, 1989, Reddick was superb in guiding the Winnipeg Jets to a 3-1 victory over Vancouver, kicking aside 35 of the 36 pucks the Canuck marksmen fired at him. It was the one puck that Reddick failed to snag with his glove or push away with his toe that placed him in a dubious NHL category: the first goaltender to appear in 100 games without recording a shutout.

So, despite having his name etched on the Stanley Cup as a member of the 1990 champion Edmonton Oilers and backstopping Fort Wayne to a perfect sweep of the 1993 IHL playoffs, Reddick may be best remembered for what he didn't do — blank an NHL opponent.

First goalie to lose 100 more games than he won

The Wrong Century Mark

1984–85

BELOW: Ron Low stands guard in the Washington Capitals' crease during another punishing night of puck panic.

I n the late 1960s, the finest team in the Manitoba Junior Hockey League was the Dauphin Kings, powerhouse team backstopped by goaltender Ron Low. The Kings went all the way to the Memorial Cup finals in 1969 and 1970, riding on the back of their goaltender and his heroic performances between the pipes.

After graduating from junior, Low went on to play for 14 professional teams in a handful of leagues, earning rookie of the year honors in the EHL and All-Star nods in the CHL. In 1978–79, Low was named the CHL's most valuable player after topping the loop with 33 wins. A member of six different NHL teams, Low had his finest year as a member of the high-flying Edmonton Oilers, recording a 17-7-1 record in 29 games.

After completing his career guarding the crease, Low went on to coach the Oilers and NY Rangers in the NHL and to serve as general manger of the IHL's Houston Aeroes, gathering positive reviews at every stop. But Low reached a new low when he became the first NHL goalie to lose 100 more games than he won.

How was this possible? Well, Mr. Low had the misfortune to be the starting goaltender for the worst expansion team ever to be granted a professional franchise. In their first three years of existence, the Caps lost 168 games. Low was the losing netminder in 94 of those matches.

Ouch! If unlucky Low had been playing in the Original Six era, he probably would have been praised for the punishment he was subjected to. After all, Al Rollins, who rolled up a 12-47-7 record for the porous Chicago Black Hawks in 1953-54 was rewarded for his courage under fire by winning the Hart Trophy as league MVP. Even Gump Worsley, who won a mitt full of Stanley Cup titles with the Montreal Canadiens, can appreciate Low's plight. The Gumper had to withstand the comical on-ice mishaps of the NY Rangers when they were even worse than the current version. Worsley, the only goalie in history to win 300 games and lose 300 games, was decorated with the ultimate honor, induction into the Hockey Hall of Fame.

First goaltender to register a shutout in his first NHL game
The Zero Hero

1926

ABOVE: Wearing his infamous "Cobra" mask, Gary Simmons' bats a loose puck out of harm's way. The designer of Simmons' mask was brilliant with the brush but clueless about cobras. If you look closely, you'll see that the reptile on Simmons' mask has rattlers!

On November 16, 1926, Hal Winkler made his NHL debut with the NY Rangers a memorable one by guiding the Broadway Blueshirts to a 1-0 victory over the Montreal Maroons. By posting the zero on the scoreboard, Winkler became the first backstopper in NHL history to record a shutout in his NHL debut. The win had an added piece of significance. It was also the first game the NY Rangers played at Madison Square Garden.

Since Winkler's impressive debut, 15 other goalies have recorded zeroes in their NHL debuts. Familiar names like Darren Puppa, Marcel Paille, Gary Simmons and Gord Henry can be found on that list, along with a few others who don't exactly flow trippingly off the tongue such as Dave Gatherum, Claude Pronovost and Andre Gil.

The newest freshman to add his name to this distinguished list is Chicago Blackhawk rookie Michael Leighton, who blanked the Phoenix Coyotes on January 8, 2003. Interestingly, Phoenix's netminder also recorded his first NHL shutout that evening in the 0-0 draw. Zac Bierk was hardly a rookie, but he had never recorded a perfect game in his NHL career. It marked the first time in NHL history that two goalies collected their first career shutouts in the same game.

Defensemen

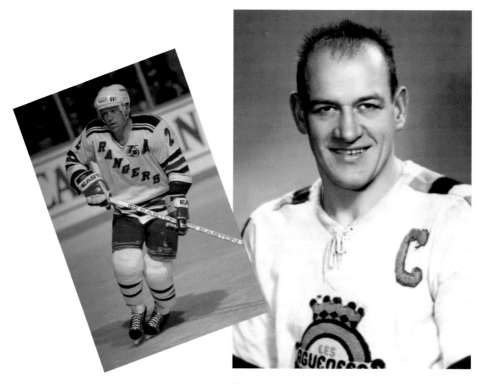

First defenseman to record 100 points in a season

A Career Year Ends a Career

1963

ABOVE: Brian Leetch is the last NHL rearguard to register 100 points in a season.

ABOVE RIGHT: Since Gerry Glaude's breakthrough 100-point season, only seven defensemen have been able to reach the century mark in points at the professional level — Mark Howe (WHA), Barry McKinlay (UHL), Bobby Orr, Denis Potvin, Paul Coffey, Al MacInnis and Brian Leetch (NHL).

As he prepared to play his 16th season in the minor leagues, Gerry Glaude knew the opportunity to make the NHL had passed him by. A gifted rearguard with a deft touch around the net and a penchant for making picture-perfect passes, Glaude scored at least ten goals six times during his career, which was a record for defensemen at the time.

In 1960, Glaude left Quebec where he had played the majority of his career and signed with the IHL's Muskegon Zephyrs, where he quickly established himself as the league's top rearguard. In the 1962–63 season, Glaude journeyed into a territory that no other defenseman had been able to enter — the Century Club. In that magical season, Glaude scored 15 goals and added 86 assists, allowing him to become the first back-liner in hockey history to collect 100 points in a single season.

Even though numerous other pro offerings were in the offing, Glaude celebrated his milestone achievement by retiring. His explanation was simple: "Too many bus trips, too little money."

First defenseman made to stop penalty shots

Hey, Ron, Stack the House!

1967

When Roger Neilson was inducted into the Hockey Hall of Fame in 2002, he was afforded the honor in recognition of the numerous coaching innovations he introduced to the game. Although he doesn't have a Stanley Cup ring on his finger yet, Neilson has always been recognized as a tactical genius.

One of his most famous ploys was introduced during the 1967–68 season while he was coaching the Peterborough Petes. During one game that season, Ron Stackhouse, a steady if somewhat plodding defenseman, pulled down an opposing forward from behind, which resulted in a penalty shot being awarded to the other team. Somehow — even Neilson admits the details have evaporated with the sands of time — Neilson came up with the wild idea of pulling the goaltender and replacing him with a defenseman.

Stackhouse was chosen to be the sacrificial lamb, as it were. Neilson's plan was simple. As soon as the opposing player touched the puck, Stackhouse would charge out of the net and check him. "We had six [penalty shots] called against us that one year and he stopped them all," Neilson recalled, with a chuckle.

Well, the Ontario Hockey League officials weren't as amused as Neilson. They quickly passed a rule mandating that a goaltender had to be in net whenever a penalty shot was taken. Ron Stackhouse remains the only non-goaltender to face a penalty shot in his career and not allow a goal. And that's one record that will never be broken.

First defenseman
to win a scoring title
From the Blueline to the Headlines

1970

By the time he was twelve years old, Robert Gordon (Bobby) Orr was already legendary in his hometown of Parry Sound, Ontario. Even at that tender age, Orr was already accomplished at dodging checks, delivering crisp and clever passes and controlling the puck. He had even perfected the half turn/spin that would be his trademark move during his brief but brilliant NHL career.

Before Orr, defensemen stayed anchored in front of the net, cleared the puck and cooked any opponent who dared enter his kitchen. Before Orr, only one defenseman in NHL history had scored 20 goals in a season. Before Orr, only one defenseman in NHL history had collected 60 points in a single season. That was before Orr destroyed the record book by registering at least 60 points in seven of his dozen years and collecting at least 20 goals in eight different seasons.

By blossoming into an offensive genius, a defensive dynamo and a relentless competitor, Orr controlled the game like no player before him. And make no mistake about it, if he had to engage in fisticuffs, Bobby would drop 'em and he could bop 'em.

In 1969–70, he became the first defenseman to collect 100 points in a season and the first — and only — rearguard to win a NHL scoring title, a feat he duplicated two years later. In 1970–71, Orr became the first player to register 100 assists in a season. At that time, only four players in the entire history of the game had recorded 100 points in a season.

Orr's #4 jersey was hoisted to the rafters and retired by the Boston Bruins on January 9, 1979, only months before he became the youngest player ever elected to the Hockey Hall of Fame. He was just 31 years old.

First defenseman to score 20 goals in a season

Who was that Flash Man?

1945

ABOVE RIGHT: Larry Sacharuk became the only defenseman in hockey history to score 50 goals in one season playing with askatoon of the Western Major Junior Hockey League.
ABOVE: Flash Hollett described his partnership with Eddie Shore this way:"I was supposed to go up and scare the attacking forwards and then Shore would hit them."

Although he occasionally played on the front line, William "Flash" Hollett put his name in the record books because of his exploits on the back line.

Blessed with blinding speed that earned him his nickname, Hollett spent much of his career as the defensive partner of Eddie Shore, the top blueliner of his generation. The lessons Hollett learned from being Shore's protégé allowed him to become the highest- scoring defenseman of his era.

Twice "Flash" notched 19 goals in a season, a mark never reached by any rearguard at the time. However, when the Bruins brass determined the club needed grit, not goals, they dispatched him to Detroit midway through the 1943–44 season for a rugged ruffian named Pat Egan. In Hollett's first full campaign in the Motor City, he became the first defenseman in hockey history to score 20 goals in a single season. It remained a NHL record until a youngster named Orr came along.

Although the 20-goal barrier has been crossed countless times, only seven NHL rearguards have been able to climb above the 30-goal mark — Paul Coffey, Bobby Orr, Denis Potvin, Kevin Hatcher, Doug Wilson, Phil Housley and Ray Bourque.

First defenseman to play every position in a single game
The King of the Rink

1923

Frank "King" Clancy was one of the most colorful characters ever to adorn a sheet of ice, a true leprechaun with a glint in his eye and an Irishman's gift of gab. He was also one of the finest rearguards ever to don a pair of skates and patrol the blueline.

King was blessed with athletic genes, so he came by his abilities honestly. There wasn't a sport invented that the King's dad couldn't master, so it shouldn't really come as a surprise that the Francis was the first player to line up as a defenseman, rover, forward and goaltender in the same NHL game.

The contest in question occurred during the 1923 Stanley Cup championship showdown between Clancy's Ottawa Senators and the Edmonton Eskimos. The series was played in Western Canada that year (it alternated from coast to coast until 1926) which meant the teams would be playing under West Coast rules and each team would have seven men on the ice.

Normally, this wouldn't pose a problem, but the Ottawa club that showed up on the left coast was a bruised and battered bunch. The team was missing four regulars, which prompted Senator bench boss T.P. Gorman to become an expert at instant improvisation.

In game four of the series, Clancy had already been employed as a defenseman, center and rover during the contest when Ottawa goaltender Clint Benedict was whistled off the ice for tripping Edmonton forward Duke Keats. At this time in the NHL, goalies served their own penalties, so a position player had to stand in the crease goal and face the punishment. Well, Clancy never met a challenge he didn't like, so he volunteered to stand between the pipes while Benedict cooled his heels in penalty-box purgatory. History tells that Clancy was superb during his brief stay in the cage, and almost scored a goal himself when he spied a loose puck and made a mad dash towards the Eskimos' net.

First defenseman to play 20 years with one team

Clapper Lights the Lamp

1947

Not only was Aubrey "Dit" Clapper the first player to suit up for 20 seasons in the NHL, he remains one of the few players to accomplish the feat while in the employ of only one team. In Clapper's case, it's just one of the many NHL firsts that adorn his resume.

Clapper wore the brown and gold of the Boston Bruins for his entire career, first as a forward, and later — when the legs lost a little of their get-up-and-go — as a defenseman. He was the first player in the history of the NHL to earn a berth on the NHL All-Star team as both a forward and a rearguard.

By the time the 1946–47 season rolled around, Clapper was the Bruins' player/coach, although he rarely suited up for action. However, on February 12, 1947, "Dit" donned his famous #5 jersey one more time and took to the ice for his final game as a NHL player. Prior to the opening face-off, Clapper was showered with gifts, cash and a thunderous ovation. The final honor awaiting the veteran Bruin was his induction into the Hockey Hall of Fame. Since he went out and played later that evening, he became the first active player to be given a berth in hockey's hallowed hall. Not even Wayne Gretzky was able to say that!

First defenseman to score five goals on five shots
Five for Five

1977

BELOW: Ian Turnbull corrals a loose puck behind the Leafs' net during the 1979-80 season. The fact that no NHL blueliner has been able to score four goals in a game since Paul Coffey plunked a quartet of pucks into the net on October 26, 1984, puts Turnbull's achievement into a proper perspective.

On February 2, 1977, Toronto defenseman Ian Turnbull's aim was true. On that eventful evening, Turnbull became the only NHL blueliner to score five goals in a game as the Leafs clipped the Red Wings 9-1. And if that wasn't special enough, Turnbull accomplished the feat by scoring on five consecutive shots.

Turnbull would have appreciated the sharpshooters who invaded the NHL during the 2002–03 season because accuracy was the name of their game. For the first time in NHL history four different players scored their first NHL goal on the only shot they took during the entire season. Toronto's Matt Stajan, who was playing junior hockey in Belleville on that day and signed by the Leafs the next, found himself in the line-up for the Leafs' final regular season game against Ottawa on April 3, 2003, and hit the bull's-eye on the first dart he threw at an enemy goaltender.

Damian Surma of the Carolina Panthers also counted his first NHL goal on his first NHL shot in a 3-1 loss to Ottawa on March 18, 2003, helping Carolina became the first team in the post-expansion era to have five different players score their first NHL goal in their first NHL game.

Zdeno Kutlak and Rickard Wallin were other sharpshooters who recorded their first NHL goal on the only shot they took during the 2002–03 campaign.

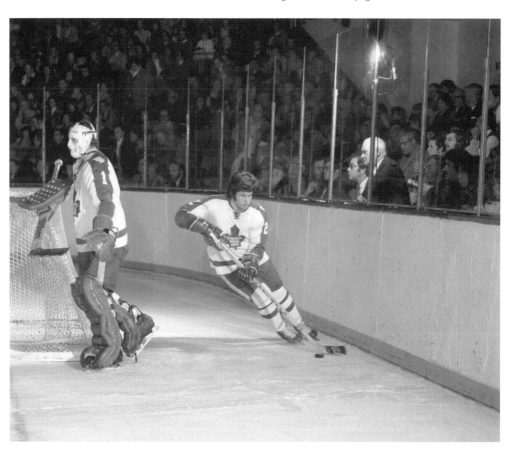

First defenseman to collect eight points in one game

Scoresheet Snowman

1977

ABOVE: Bill Barber (7) keeps a close eye on Toronto's Tiger Williams (22) while Philly defenseman Tom Bladon stands guard in front of the Flyers' crease. Bladon's record of eight points by a rearguard has never been beaten, though Paul Coffey equaled it with two goals and six assists in Edmonton's 12-3 win over Detroit on March 14, 1984.

Tom Bladon had a night for the ages and a slot for the record book on December 11, 1977, when he recorded four goals and added four assists in the Philadelphia Flyers' 11-1 whipping of the Cleveland Barons. Since Bladon finished the season with only 11 goals and 35 points, he collected 25 percent of his season's output in a single game! There's not another player who ever donned a jersey and skated in the NHL who can make that claim.

And no other player can match the evening Gordon "Red" Berenson enjoyed as a member of the St. Louis Blues on November 7, 1968. The Blues were in Philadelphia for a tilt with the Flyers and Berenson felt like he was on a roll. The first player to go directly from the US college system to the NHL, Berenson had never scored more than seven goals in his first six NHL seasons with the Montreal Canadiens. When the NHL expanded in 1967, the Red Baron was selected by the St. Louis Blues. In his first season, he led the team with 22 goals. But on this night, he would place his name in the record book. And it's still there.

Berenson lit the lamp six times against a pair of Flyers goalies, becoming the only NHL player to record a double hat-trick in a road game. One other aspect of the evening was unique. Berenson scored every goal in five-on-five situations. That is also a first. And it may also be a last.

Pioneers

First Black player to play hockey
Breaking the Color Barrier

1958

ABOVE: When
Washington's Mike Marson
made his NHL debut
on October 9, 1974, he
became only the second
Black athlete (and the first
in 14 years) to play in the
NHL.

ABOVE RIGHT: Even the
most ardent hockey advo-
cates may not know that
Willie O'Ree played the
majority of his career with
only one eye. While playing
with Kitchener/Waterloo
of the Ontario Junior
League during the 1955-56
season, O'Ree lost 95
percent of the vision in
his right eye when a stray
puck clipped him in the face.

The first athlete to break the NHL "color barrier" was a
smooth-skating, clever stick-handler from Fredericton, New
Brunswick, with a touch of Irish in his name and a bit of the
blarney in his game. Willie O'Ree's road to the show began
when he signed his first pro contract to play for the Quebec
Aces, one of the most storied franchises in the old Quebec Senior
Hockey League. When O'Ree signed on, the club was affiliated with
the Boston Bruins, which afforded him the opportunity to attend
his first NHL training camp. The Beantown brass liked the youngster's poise under pressure and told him that he could be the first
of his race to make it to the NHL.

When the Bruins found themselves rocked with injuries
midway through the 1957–58 campaign, the call went out for
O'Ree. On January 18, 1958, in the fabled Montreal Forum,
he became the first Black player to skate in the NHL.

While O'Ree may have been the first Black player to
ascend to the NHL, he was hardly the first to play the game.
In 1899, Hipple "Hippo" Galloway became the first Black athlete
to play in an organized league when he took a turn with
Woodstock in the Central Ontario Hockey Association.

The first Black athlete to climb the corporate ladder and
land in the front office of a professional hockey club was John
Paris Jr., of Windsor, Nova Scotia. Paris was the first Black to
become a head coach and general manager when he took
over the reins of the ECHL's Macon Whoopee in 1997.

The first All-Black hockey league
A League of Their Own

1900

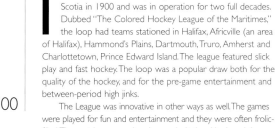

The Only All-Colored Hockey Team in Canada

he first All-Black hockey league was established in Nova Scotia in 1900 and was in operation for two full decades. Dubbed "The Colored Hockey League of the Maritimes," the loop had teams stationed in Halifax, Africville (an area of Halifax), Hammond's Plains, Dartmouth, Truro, Amherst and Charlottetown, Prince Edward Island. The league featured slick play and fast hockey. The loop was a popular draw both for the quality of the hockey, and for the pre-game entertainment and between-period high jinks.

The League was innovative in other ways as well. The games were played for fun and entertainment and they were often frolic-filled. The matches were played on an invitational basis and there was no championship trophy awaiting the winners. But make no mistake, the skill level was high and the competition could be fierce. Like the Harlem Globetrotters, the players knew when to cut out the shenanigans and get down to business. It was family fun and it worked, keeping the seats full for over two decades.

First player to get
$1,000,000 to play hockey

If You Pay It, He Will Come

1972

BELOW TOP: "My wife made me a millionaire. Before she divorced me, I had three million."— Bobby Hull, on what signing the first seven-figure contract in hockey history really meant.

BELOW BOTTOM: In 1972, Gerry Cheevers deserted the financially tight-fisted Boston Bruins and cashed in with the WHA's Cleveland Crusaders.

BELOW RIGHT: Derek "Turk" Sanderson signed a multi-million dollar deal with the WHA's Philadelphia Blazers in 1972, but when he failed to fill the rink and the net, he was unceremoni-ously dispatched back to Boston after playing only eight games.

When the WHA first contacted Bobby Hull about the possibility of having him join their new league, Hull threw out a cash demand that he was certain this fledgling league could never match by saying, "Give me a million dollars and I'll play." Never in a million years did he expect to have his demand honored.

However, the WHA brass knew they needed a superstar to give the league credibility, so each of the WHA franchises chipped in the cash and Hull was given his $1,000,000.

The WHA spent their first summer throwing money around like confetti, signing other such NHL stars as Parent, Cheevers, Sanderson, McKenzie and Tremblay to lavish multi-million dollar deals. For most of those players, the contracts were worth about as much as the pens used to sign them and very few of the former NHLers actually saw the money promised them.

But Hull not only saw this cash, he got it all in one lovely lump sum. And that made him the first $1,000,000 athlete — not only in hockey, in all of pro sports.

First team to travel by air
Fly Me to the Rink...

1935

When Colonel John Hammond, the president of the NY Rangers, decided that the easiest way to get his weary team of Rangers from New York to Toronto and home again would be by air, he commissioned the Curtis-Wright Corporation to transport his club to and from Toronto via airplane. It marked the first time a NHL team used aviation as a means of transportation.

It's a good thing Hammond wasn't a superstitious man. The team was scheduled to depart on Friday the 13th, which was not a promising omen. However, the team arrived and departed without mishap except for the score, which went into the record books as a 6-5 win for the Leafs and a loss, on the ice and in the budget, for the Broadway-bound Blueshirts.

First best-selling author to play goal in the NHL

From Paper to Pads

1977

Prior to the start of the 1977–78 season, George Plimpton, a renowned author, humorist and occasional actor, submitted a rather odd request to the brass of the Boston Bruins. Plimpton, who already tackled the tough task of playing quarterback for the Detroit Lions (as documented in his #1 best-seller *Paper Lion*) and tossed up schoolyard curveballs to the top sluggers in major league baseball, wanted to take a turn in nets for the Bruins. Sensing a potential publicity extravaganza, Boston agreed to allow the tall, wafer-thin author to attend training camp and spend five minutes in the crease during an exhibition game against the roughest, toughest on-ice hombres in the NHL, the Philadelphia "Broad Street Bullies" Flyers.

Not only did Plimpton survive — he actually stopped a well-orchestrated penalty shot during his tenure in net. He later wrote about his experiences, concentrating more on the characters he encountered, like roommate Jim Beattie and Bruins bench boss Don Cherry, than his waddling "ankles-on-ice" skating style.

Plimpton's book may have sold piles, but the all-time chart-topping tome written by a goalie was penned by Ken Dryden, the academically inclined, introspective Hall of Fame netminder.

First North American to play in Russia

Oh, Oh, I'm not at Harvard Anymore!

1990–91

BELOW: "I walked away convinced more than ever that the Soviet people are the same as you and I — people who want to be accepted. People who have the same feelings and needs we do."—Tod Hartje.

BELOW RIGHT: Vincent Riendeau was the first NHL player from North America to play in Russia, but he wasn't the last. In 2002-03, seven former NHL stars — Chris Wells, David Cooper, Bruce Gardiner, Mike Fountain, Martin Brochu, Patrick Labrecque and Marcel Cousineau — were playing in Russia.

When most pundits are asked who the first North American player to lace 'em up in the Russian Elite Leagues was, they usually refer to goaltender Vincent Riendeau, who covered the crease for the Lada Togliatti club from 1998 to 2000. While it's true that Riendeau was the first player with NHL experience to tackle the culture shock, customs and cuisine as an everyday member of a Russian team, he wasn't the first North American to actually play hockey professionally in Russia.

No, that honor goes to Tod Hartje, a native of Anoka, Minnesota, and a graduate of Harvard University. Hartje was drafted by the Winnipeg Jets, whose general manager was Mike Smith, a vocal supporter of European hockey and an expert in Russian hockey history. In the NHL of the early 1990s, Mr. Smith's opinions on the importance of the European style of playing the game weren't exactly welcomed by other members of the NHL's boardroom brass, but Smith continued to find new ways to combine both hockey philosophies.

One of the projects Smith proposed was sending a Winnipeg prospect to play in Russia. Hartje wasn't a prize jewel in the Jets' system, but he was an intelligent, rational, hard-working and intuitive player whose powers of observation would go beyond what he saw on the ice surface. In the fall of 1990, Hartje relocated to Russia, and he spent the entire 1990–91 season playing with Sokol Kiev. Smith's instincts about Hartje were accurate. When he returned home, he documented his trials, tribulations, observations and opinions as the first Yank to play Soviet hockey in a book entitled, *From Behind the Red Line — A North American Hockey Player in Russia.*

European Invasion

First player from Finland
to play in the NHL
The Flying Finn

1947

ABOVE: After retiring
as an active player, Pentti
Lund remained in Port
Arthur/Fort William
(Thunder Bay), eventually
becoming the sports editor
of the *Times-News* morning
newspaper.

Pentti Lund was the first Northern-European-born player in the NHL. A native of Helsinki, Finland, Lund and his family moved to Canada in 1931 when he was six years old.

Lund joined the Bruins during the Stanley Cup finals after leading the EHL in scoring with 92 points during the 1946-47 season. Although he made his NHL debut with Boston, his finest years in the NHL came as a member of the NY Rangers. He captured the Calder Trophy in 1948–49 as the loops best newcomer, becoming the second consecutive European-born player to be named NHL rookie of the year. Jimmy McFadden, a native of Belfast, Ireland, won the award in 1947–48.

The first Finnish born and trained player to become a member of the Hockey Hall of Fame was Jari Kurrii, the sweet-shooting sniper who was a scoring sensation with the Edmonton Oilers in their dynasty years during the 1980s. Kurri was a member of five Stanley Cup-winning teams and is the NHL's all-time leading European-trained player with 601 goals and 1398 points.

First European-trained player in North America

Sterner Storms

1964

BELOW: Ulf Sterner accepts a ceremonial goblet in recognition of his achievements in international hockey and ground-breaking appearance with the AHL's Baltimore Clippers and the NHL's NY Rangers.
BOTTOM: Sterner as a member of the NY Rangers.

The first European-trained player to make it to the NHL was Ulf Sterner, a member of the Swedish National Team who was a standout at the 1963 World Championships. Invited to join the NY Rangers at their training camp in September of 1963, Sterner's performance was impressive enough to earn him a five-game NHL trial. But the International Ice Hockey Federation (IIHF) threatened to strip him of his amateur status if he played a professional game, so Sterner postponed his North American debut until the conclusion of the 1964 Winter Olympics.

In September of 1964, Sterner attended the Rangers' training camp again and was assigned to the club's main AHL farm team in Baltimore. Despite some early success, the experience was an unpleasant one for Sterner. After making his NHL debut on January 27, 1965, in a game against the Boston Bruins, Sterner saw action in three more games with the Rangers, but his ice time was limited. At the conclusion of the season, he returned to Sweden and signed to play with Vastra Frolunda, a Division II team in the Swedish Elite League.

First Iron Curtain player to play in North America
Czech, Please!

BELOW TOP: Jaroslav Jirik during his brief stay with the St. Louis Blues.
BOTTOM: Stan Mikita, who was born in Czechoslovakia but raised in Canada, was the first player in NHL history to win three major awards in the same season when he captured the Hart, Art Ross and Lady Byng awards in 1966-67.

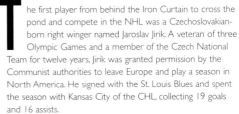

The first player from behind the Iron Curtain to cross the pond and compete in the NHL was a Czechoslovakian-born right winger named Jaroslav Jirik. A veteran of three Olympic Games and a member of the Czech National Team for twelve years, Jirik was granted permission by the Communist authorities to leave Europe and play a season in North America. He signed with the St. Louis Blues and spent the season with Kansas City of the CHL, collecting 19 goals and 16 assists.

After Kansas City failed to make the playoffs, Jirik was promoted to the Blues and appeared in three games, against Chicago, Los Angeles and Oakland. When Jirik returned home after that season, he disclosed the fact he had married an American woman, which would have given him the right to stay in the United States. As a valuable member of the Czech National Team, hockey officials were worried Jirik would defect, so they refused him permission to return to North America, although he had been invited to return for training camp in 1970–71. So Jirik remained overseas and played for ZKL Brno of the Czech National League until 1975.

The first non-North American player to win the NHL's Art Ross Trophy was a native of Czechoslovakia. In 1994–95, Jaromir Jagr won the first of his five NHL scoring titles, collecting 70 points in 48 games.

First Russian-trained player in the NHL
Unnatural Nechaev

1982

The first Russian-trained athlete to play in the NHL was Victor Nechaev, who was selected by the Los Angeles Kings in the seventh round of the 1982 Entry Draft. His story is packed with enough political intrigue, sexual ambiguity and behind-the-scenes conspiracies to fill any contemporary spy novel.

In 1981, Nechaev met an American student named Cheryl Haigler who was traveling through the Soviet Union. Despite cultural and language differences, they had a whirlwind romance and were married. She returned to the USA when her visa expired but it took Nechaev several months to obtain his "release" from the Soviet officials.

Yet, instead of going to Boston where his wife was living, Nechaev headed west to Los Angeles, where his cousin ran a Russian-language TV and radio station. Once he arrived in Tinseltown, Nechaev met up with Kings' g.m. George Maguire and asked for a tryout. Maguire gave him a quick look-see and was impressed enough to select him in the 1982 draft. Nechaev showed promise in training camp and earned a berth with the New Haven Nighthawks of the AHL, where he registered 11 points in 28 games. He also appeared in three games for the Kings, scoring his first — and only — NHL goal. From all reports he was a contentious fellow, and when he balked at returning to the minors after his brief tour of duty with the Kings, he was released.

First Russian-trained athlete allowed to play in the NHL

Fast Actin' Priakin

1989

ABOVE: Calgary's signing of Sergei Priakin ushered in a new era in the history of professional hockey. Within weeks of Priakin's NHL debut, three of the greatest players in Russian hockey history signed contracts with NHL teams. Calgary inked Sergei Makarov, New Jersey signed Slava Fetisov, while the Vancouver Canucks reached terms with Igor Larionov.

When an unassuming and relatively unknown player by the name of Sergei Priakin suited up with the Calgary Flames at the conclusion of the 1988–89 season, it marked a changing of the guard in the NHL philosophy. Priakin was the first Russian-trained player to come to North America and play in the NHL with the full support and blessing of the Soviet Ice Hockey Federation. While Priakin didn't make a great impact in the league as a player, his appearance marked the beginning of the Iron Curtain invasion, an influx of talented players that made the NHL the world's first truly global professional sports organization.

Only weeks after Priakin's NHL debut, the Soviet Union's news agency Tass announced that three players from the elite "Big Red Army," one of the finest on-ice units ever assembled, were being released by the club and were free to pursue professional opportunities in North America. The trio — Slava Fetisov, Sergei Makarov and Igor Larionov — were not only members of the team, they were among the greatest players the USSR had ever produced. Other key members of the once dominant Soviet team followed, including Sergei Starikov, Helmut Balderis and Sergei Mylnikov.

Perhaps the media put it best when the headlines read, "The Russians are coming, the Russians are coming," adapting the title of a famous 1960s film directed by Canadian Norman Jewison about a entirely different kind of invasion.

First European scouted in the phone book

Let Your Fingers Do the Walking

1973

BELOW: Although he was a decidedly old-school coach and general manager, even Punch Imlach had to eventually acquiesce and admit that the European-trained players were not only skilled and crafty, they were also durable.

This is actually the story of a player who never existed. In the early days of the draft, teams could use another team's pick if that team didn't care to make a selection. But that dog didn't hunt, as far as Punch Imlach, the Buffalo Sabres' crusty general manager was concerned. Punch had an authoritarian attitude that wouldn't allow him to let any team take advantage of his generosity, so he selected a "player" named Taro Tsujimoto, 183rd overall in the 1973 Amateur Draft. It wasn't until years later that Imlach disclosed that while Mr. Tsujimoto existed, it was quite doubtful he had ever laced on a pair of skates. Imlach had let his fingers do the walking through the Buffalo phone book and had chosen Tsujimoto's name at random. Punch, who was known to pay off his bets in pennies and single dollar bills, just couldn't allow anyone to get the better of him.

As odd as that draft year and that draft selection was, it pales in comparison to the 1983 NHL Entry Draft, which was the first and only year that an existing NHL franchise did not select a single player.

It was a season of turmoil in St. Louis. The team was in financial chaos and actually were without an owner for a period of time. A group from Saskatchewan led by "Wild" Bill Hunter attempted to purchase the franchise, but the NHL was reluctant to relocate a team to such a small market area, preferring to find local ownership. So when draft day arrived, and the future of the franchise was in flux, the club did not select any of the available players.

There is a certain irony involved in this tale. When the NHL expanded in 1967, St. Louis was awarded a franchise even though they didn't have anyone submit a real bid. What the NHL did have was a powerful owner in Chicago's Bill Wirtz, whose family also owned an arena in St. Louis that was begging for an tenant. Wirtz called in a marker, the city received an NHL franchise and then the NHL found an owner.

First NHL player strike
Shut it Down

1925

BELOW: Shorty Green, as a member of the famed "Tiger line" of the New York Americans, scored the first goal in the new Madison Square Garden during the 1925–26 season.
BOTTOM: The Hamilton Tigers were led by future Hall of Fame member Billy Burch and school boy star Shorty Green. During the 1920s the downtown area in Hamilton featured drinking fountains with green water. The ones that still exist are called "shorty greens" by local old timers.

"Professional hockey is a money-making affair. The promoters are in the game for what they can make out of it and the players wouldn't be in the game if they didn't look at matters in the same light."

With these rabble-rousing words from Shorty Green, he and future Hall of Fame member Billy Burch led their 1925 Hamilton Tigers team on a post-season strike that cost each player a chance to win the Stanley Cup. Burch, who scored 20 goals in 27 games to win the Hart Trophy that season, teamed with wingers Shorty and Red Green to form an unstoppable line, making the Tigers a Cup favorite.

Who's to say whether the player strike was business or greed? The NHL had expanded the season from 24 to 30 games and increased the playoff format. Two new expansion clubs, Boston Bruins and Montreal Maroons, had joined the NHL in 1924, paying other club owners $15,000 for the privilege of joining them. Amid the increased profits, the players on the playoff-bound Hamilton Tigers wanted a cash bonus of $200 per man. After all, other clubs had acknowledged the additional workload by paying bonuses and raising salaries. But not Hamilton and their general manager, Percy Thompson.

Despite several days of negotiations, the players refused to budge and so Thompson enlisted NHL president Frank Calder, who threatened to suspend the players. The players, in turn, threatened never to skate again for Hamilton. The playoffs came and went with Montreal defeating Toronto for the NHL title. Victoria of the Western Hockey League won the Stanley Cup over Montreal and had their name inscribed on the trophy. The Hamilton Tigers, the best team in the league, sat at home suspended and unpaid.

Hamilton ownership understood the players' resolve and sold the club for $75,000 to Bill Dwyer, who had made his fortune in bootleg whisky. The team headed south for the Big Apple, and became the New York Americans. Billy Burch got a three-year deal for $25,000 and Shorty Green received a 40% pay raise. But neither man ever came close to the Cup again, and the striking players were forced to apologize to the league in writing.

First player lockout to last 300 days

It's Not a Strike

2004-05

BELOW: With no play on ice, hockey fans turned to their past. The 2004 induction class included Ray Bourque, Paul Coffey, Larry Murphy, and Cliff Fletcher, shown here answering questions at the Hockey Hall of Fame Induction Fan Forum.

BOTTOM: Through the trying days of hockey's longest play stoppage, Commissioner Gary Bettman stood steadfast as the representative of hockey to millions of fans.

A lot of people say that in this type of situation nobody wins. But that's never true. It's about control and the owners got what they wanted—control."

Ron MacLean, host of Hockey Night in Canada, summed up the longest player strike/lockout in the history of professional sports in North America with words about winning and control. The lockout, which began September 15, 2004, cost fans, players, and owners 1,230 regular-season games plus the 2005 Stanley Cup playoffs. The bone of contention was "cost certainty." In other words, a "salary cap." With the new CBA (contract between the players union and owners), hockey joined professional football by instituting a rigid cap on player salaries—the greatest expense in a team budget. Some of the results of the agreement that followed the 301-day lockout included:

1. The union had the right to re-negotiate the current six-year contract after the fourth year.
2. 24% salary rollback on all existing player contracts.
3. Team-by-team salary cap based on projected revenues of $1.8 billion.
4. No player could earn more than 20% of the team cap. For 2005-06, this meant no player could earn more than $7.4 million.
5. The league's total expenditure on player costs could not exceed 54% of hockey-related revenue.
6. A rookie salary cap of $850,000 with players entering the league receiving free agency after seven years.
7. The age of unrestricted free agency remained 31 but would be brought down to 27 by the end of 2007-08 season.
8. Teams could buy players out of their contracts at 2/3 their value if they needed to fit under the cap. Clubs would not be able to resign those players.
9. Revenue-sharing where the top 10 money-making clubs contributed to a fund shared by the bottom 10 teams.
10. Salary arbitration for both players and owners. Previously only the players had that right.
11. NHL participation in the 2006 Torino Winter Olympics.

While the monetary sacrifice was huge, owners used the impasse to implement rule changes that benefited both the players and fans. Some of those changes were merely enforcing rules that already existed, such as zero tolerance for hooking, holding, tripping, slashing, cross checking, and interference. The result was more hockey being played with less fighting.

Tie games were to be decided by shootouts. Overtime with 4-on-4 play would follow a regulation tie. Then, if there was no winner, the two teams would go to a college style shootout, which was the same as everyday practice but with an arena full of fans to watch.

The two-line pass was made legal. This brought the NHL into line with European, International, and college hockey, and added more excitement with long passes leading to breakaway scores.

New restrictions on goalies included down-sizing leg pads, blockers, catching gloves, and jerseys as well as declaring the size of the goalie-restricted-area to just behind the net. Goalies had been ranging, protected by interference rules, far from the net and playing like defensemen. Now, their area of immunity had been reduced.

So who won? The players were again playing and many were making salaries in excess of $1 million, while the owners now had some idea of what their future costs would be. And the fans had their game back.

First hockey team with brains
Road's Scholars

As many of these stories will attest, you don't have to be a Rhodes Scholar to play hockey. But that doesn't mean Rhodes Scholars can't play hockey! Over the years, the Oxford University Hockey Team has featured some of the greatest intellectual and influential minds of our time in their lineup. The sands of time have eroded many of their accomplishments on the ice, but nothing could erase the contributions they made outside the arena. Here are just a few of the exemplary talented men who traded in their skates for statesmanship and scholarship.

The Right Honorable Lester B. "Mike" Pearson
Nobel Peace Prize recipient and former Canadian prime minister.

The Honorable Dr. George Stanley
Designer of Canada's flag and former lieutenant-governor of New Brunswick.

Clarence Campbell
Former NHL referee, former NHL president and a prosecuting attorney at the Nuremberg Trials.

The Right Honorable Roland "Roly" Michener
Former Canadian governor-general.

General Peter Dawkins
The 1958 Heisman Trophy Winner and American brigadier-one star general.

The Honorable Allan Blakeney
Premier of Saskatchewan from 1971 to 1982.

Paul Almond
Award-winning author (*High Hopes, Coming of Age at the Mid Century*) as well as a noted film and television director.

R.H.G "Dick" Bonnycastle
A well-known "Gentleman Adventurer" who also founded Harlequin Books and became the first mayor of Greater Winnipeg, Manitoba.

Major Talbot Papineau
Known as Canada's "Lost Leader," he was posthumously awarded the Military Cross after being killed in action at the Battle of Passchendaele in 1917. Major Papineau was featured in Sandra Gwyn's "Tapestry of War" and was honored in the Governor General's Eulogy for Canada's Unknown Soldier on May 28, 2000.

RIGHT: Lester Pearson and Roland Michener both played for the Oxford University team.

BELOW: This spry, high-stepping gentleman is Roland Michener, who spent three seasons as a member of the Oxford University hockey team (1921-1923) and served as the Governor General of Canada from 1967 to 1974.

BELOW RIGHT: Lester B. "Mike" Pearson, a team-mate of Michener's on the Oxford hockey team, won the Nobel Peace Prize in 1957 for his role in settling the Suez Canal crisis. In 1963, he became Canada's fourteenth prime minister.

E.A. Nanton   L.M. "Mike" Pearson   K.E. "Ken" Taylor   D.R. "Roly" Michener   F.M. Bacon III
R.H.G. "Dick" Bonnycastle   E.B. Pitblado (Captain)   J.C. "Jack" Farthing   Ron McCall

First European to be hired as a head coach in the NHL

What Kind of Fool Am I?

BELOW: Alpo Suhonen behind the bench of the Chicago Blackhawks.
BOTTOM: The hiring of Suhonen (far right) didn't open many doors. Czech-born Ivan Hlinka is the only other European to serve as a head coach in the NHL.

Alpo Suhonen has a lengthy list of firsts tacked on his impressive resume, and not all of them are exclusive to the sport of hockey. Suhonen had already carved a spot in the archives when Mike Smith, the g.m. of the Chicago Blackhawks appointed him as the first European-born and trained head coach in NHL history on May 22, 2000.

Suhonen and Smith had a long and successful relationship as authors, as friends, as partners, and as hockey analysts. It was Smith, then the g.m. of the Winnipeg Jets, who hired Suhonen to be the first European-born and trained assistant coach in NHL history. That hiring prompted CBC hockey's main talking head and off-color guy Don Cherry — whose distaste for anything European, especially hockey talent, is legendary — to spew one of his most famous lines, comparing Suhonen's first name to a brand of dog food.

An intuitive and introspective man who forged a successful career for himself in Finland as a theater director, Suhonen was the perfect partner for Winnipeg Jets' general manager Mike Smith. No North American hockey executive believed and trusted the European hockey philosophy more than Smith, as the story in this volume about Tod Hartje will testify. Smith, like Suhonen, believed that coaching professional sports could be approached from an intellectual angle, even if the students, the players in this case, weren't interested in attending class. By utilizing a coaching philosophy that concentrated on the individual and getting the optimum performance out of the player, Smith and Suhonen were confident that a team dynamic would appear naturally, without the blackboards, lecturing, scolding and physical discipline. Although the plan was ideal when viewed on paper, it was a failure where it truly counted — on the ice, in the standings and in the bank account.

Near the end of a mostly disastrous first season, Suhonen developed a serious heart condition that forced him to step down as the coach of the team with only seven games left on the schedule. He returned to Finland and continues to coach his way.

First Russian player to be drafted by the NHL

I'm Always the Last to Know

ABOVE: The first Russian-born goaltender to be drafted by a NHL team, Vladislav Tretiak (#20) never had the opportunity to play in the NHL. By the time the Soviet hockey federation allowed players to sign with North American clubs, Tretiak was too old. His excellence was recognized when he became the first Soviet-trained player to be inducted into the Hockey Hall of Fame. Tretiak's teammates Slava Fetisov (#2) and Alexei Kasatanov did go on to play in the NHL.

A skilled skater and clever stickhandler, Viktor Khatulev was a member of the Soviet Junior team that captured the gold medal in the first two World Junior tournaments that were ever played. In the 1974 series, which was played in Leningrad, Khatulev was the leading scorer. The following year the competition moved to Winnipeg, and Khatulev was easily the star of the show, gaining a berth on the First All-Star Team and earning the Top Forward Award.

Although neither competition was sanctioned by the International Ice Hockey Federation and the results were considered "unofficial," the high quality of play and the fierce competitive spirit were instrumental factors in forcing the IIHF to establish an official junior world championship in 1977.

Khatulev's impressive showing on the North American stage caught the eye of a number of NHL scouts. In the 1975 Amateur Draft, he was selected by the Philadelphia Flyers in the seventh round, becoming the first Soviet-born and -trained player to be drafted by a NHL team.

Khatulev didn't even know he had been drafted until 1978. In 1975, he was suspended by the Russian Hockey Federation for five years for fighting. Many pundits believe that the suspension was enforced because Khatulev refused to leave Latvia to play for the Red Army team in Moscow when he was requested to do so.

With his hockey career in limbo, Khatulev lost both his will and his skill. He worked menial jobs as a taxi driver and warehouse laborer, struggled with alcohol and eventually died at age 39. His body was found in a back alley of the very city he decided not to play hockey in — Moscow.

Other notable European firsts
The Cross-Atlantic Crusaders

BELOW: Czech mates — Peter, Anton and Marion Stastny defected from Czechoslovakia, moved to Canada and signed with the Quebec Nordiques.

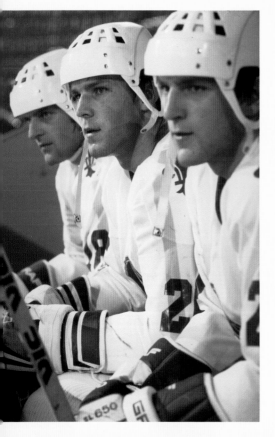

First player to represent three different countries in International competition
Peter Stastny represented Czechoslovakia (World Championships), Canada (Canada Cup Tournament) and Slovakia (Olympics) during his lengthy Hall-of-Fame career.

First German player to be drafted by the NHL
Bernhard Englbrecht was Atlanta Flames 11th pick in the 1978 NHL Amateur Draft.

First Czechoslovakian player to be drafted by the NHL
Ladislav Svozil was Detroit Red Wings 14th pick in the 1978 NHL Amateur Draft.

First European player to be drafted by the NHL
Tommi Salmelainen was St Louis Blues 5th pick in the 1969 NHL Amateur Draft.

First Russian-born player to play in the NHL
Val Hoffinger was born on January 1, 1903, in Seltz, Russia, but grew up in Salvador, Saskatchewan.

The first player born in Argentina to be drafted by the NHL
Goaltender John Wrigley was born on January 30, 1946, in Buenos Aires. He was signed by Los Angeles Kings in 1967 but never played in the NHL.

The first player born in Greece to be drafted by the NHL
Right-winger Pete Mavroudis was born on March 3, 1958, in Florina. He played with the IHL's Dayton & Grand Rapids franchises in the 1970s.

The first player born in New Zealand to be drafted by the NHL
Center Bill MacNaught was born on December 25, 1958, in Wellington. He played with the IHL's Fort Wayne Komets in the 1970s.

The first player born in Rhodesia to be drafted by the NHL
Cal Russell was born on November 10, 1949, in Salisbury, which today is called Harare. He was signed by Minnesota North Stars in 1970, but never did play. Rhodesia is known as Zimbabwe today.

The first player born in Trinidad to be drafted by the NHL
Sam Gellard was born on May 14, 1950, in Port of Spain. He played for both the WHA's Philadelphia Blazers and the Vancouver Blazers between 1972 and 1974.

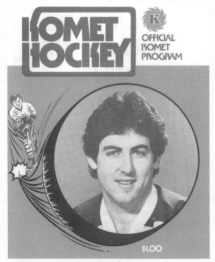

1979-80 SEASON · Our 28th Consecutive Year

TOP: Goalmouth action during the 2002 Salt Lake City Olympic Games.
ABOVE: New Zealand native, Bill MacNaught.

RIGHT: Sam Gellard was raised in Truro, Nova Scotia.

Chicks with Sticks

First female to play in a professional men's hockey league
Not Just Another Pretty Face

1992

ABOVE: Cammi Granato, the all-time leading scorer in the history of the USA women's hockey program, fires a shot towards Team Canada goalie Manon Rheaume. Granato's brother, Tony, is the head coach of the NHL's Colorado Avalanche.

P hil Esposito, general manager of the Tampa Bay Lightning, opened the door on a new threshold of hockey history when he signed free-agent female goaltender Manon Rheaume to a professional contract on August 8, 1992. Rheaume, who had already earned a place in the halls of hockey folklore when she became the first woman to play Major Junior hockey with Trois-Rivieres during the 1991–92 season, certainly had legitimate hockey talent. She was athletic, sincere, motivated and had inherited hearty hockey genes (her brother Pascal is still an active NHL player). She was also very attractive.

For most skeptics, Esposito just needed an innovative idea to generate some off-ice attention for his floundering team. Rheaume's appearance at the Tampa Bay training camp that fall was met with derision from almost every member of her male hockey brethren. Jim Kyte, a former NHL defenseman who is now a columnist for the *Ottawa Citizen*, recalls his reaction: "As a player, I scoffed at the promotional stunt. There were other legitimate players who had worked extremely hard for many years just to get an opportunity at an NHL training camp."

For his part, Espo played his trump card like a wily Las Vegas high roller. The Lightning were front-page news for weeks, and when Esposito allowed Rheaume to play the first period of an exhibition game against the St. Louis Blues on September 23, 1992, the ratings hit the roof.

The diminutive goaltender went on to play for several seasons on the minor league circuit, including a brief sojourn in Las Vegas where the aforementioned Mr. Kyte was serving as team captain. Kyte admits that while the lads did fire a few "high and hard" ones over, under, and right at Rheaume's head in practice, their hard-line stance softened when they realized she had a relentless dedication to discipline and detail.

"The bottom line was that she may not have had the right to be there from a skill viewpoint," he observed, "but she won her teammates over with her positive attitude, outstanding work ethic and professionalism."

The first female goaltender to win a professional game
A Win for All Women

1993

Sure, cynics scoffed that Manon Rheaume was a publicity toy. But even the most hardened scribe had to take notice when four-time Eastern College Athletic Conference All-Conference goaltender Erin Whitten became the first female goaltender to win a game in a minor professional league.

Whitten, the first female goalie to play in the AHL when she attended to crease duties with the Adirondack Red Wings during an exhibition game prior to the 1993–94 season, recorded the victory on October 30, 1993, as a member of the East Coast Hockey League's Toledo Storm. Called into duty midway through a game against the Dayton Bombers, Whitten backstopped the Storm to a 6-5 win.

During the 1995–96 season, Whitten was a member of the Colonial Hockey League's Flint Generals when she made history again. In one of her final professional appearances, Whitten "went all the way," becoming the first female to play and win an entire regular-season game as her Generals marched to a 6-5 victory over the Detroit Falcons.

First female to play professional hockey as a forward

Up Front with the Guys

2003

In the early months of 2003, the hockey pages of every major newspaper were crammed with columns concerning the exploits of Hayley Wickenheiser, perhaps the finest female forward ever to play the sport. A member of the Canadian National Women's Team since 1994 and a cousin of former first overall NHL draft selection Doug Wickenheiser, the 5'9" fireplug made headlines when she signed a 30-day tryout contract with Kirkkonummi Salamat, a team in Finland's Second Division.

More than 84 scribes and media types applied for accreditation to witness, discuss, debate and report on her first game. Normally, only the local newspaper would be on hand to report on the match. Wickenheiser, who became the first female hockey player to register a point in a professional league when she recorded an assist in her pro debut on January 11, 2003, later signed a contract to play the remainder of 2002–03 season. On February 1, 2003, she became the first female to score a goal in a men's pro league.

While there can be doubt that Wickenheiser is capable of playing the "big boys," she wasn't the first female to play forward in a professional men's league.

That accolade goes to Maren Valenti, who played 24 games for EHC Freiburg of Germany's second division during the 1998–99 season. Valenti only averaged around six minutes a game and she wasn't able to register a point during her time with the team.

But don't doubt the nature of the competition that she faced just to make that team. The roster that season included former NHL players Greg Andrusak, Mario Bruneta, Andrew McKim, Magnus Roupe and Thomas Steen, all of whom forged fine careers for themselves in the world's greatest hockey league.

First female hockey player in *Time* and *Newsweek*

Yuppie, That's Abby

1956

In the mid-1950s, Toronto's Abigail (Abby) Hoffman was a keen and talented eight-year-old hockey player. The trouble was, there was nowhere for her to play competitive hockey. So, Abigail cut her hair, registered herself as "Ab" Hoffman and played defense on a boy's team for the entire season. Her only problem was that she was too good. "Ab" was selected to join an All-Star team that was slated to play in numerous top-notch tournaments. However, because of the elite nature of the competition, there were strict regulations concerning age and birthplace. That meant Abby had to resubmit her birth certificate before she could suit up with the team. When she did, the truth was uncovered and Hoffman was immediately suspended from further play.

Abby and her family filed a lawsuit fighting for the league to allow her to continue playing, but the Ontario Supreme Court upheld the league's decision and her blossoming hockey career came to an end. But it wasn't the end of the story.

Various North American periodicals picked up the story, including both *Time Magazine* and *Newsweek*, and the publicity paved the way for the establishment of the first organized hockey league for girls.

Hoffman later became one of Canada's greatest female track and field athletes, competing in four Olympiads. In 1976, she was selected to be Canada's flag-bearer at the first Olympic Games held in Canada.

The first women's hockey game
Out of the Kitchen and onto the Ice

1891

Much like the origins of the game itself, there are varying accounts as to when and where the first "recorded" game of women's ice hockey was played.

Total Hockey, the official encyclopedia of the NHL, claims that the first game between all-women teams was played in Ottawa, where the Government House team defeated the Rideau team in 1889. This is a credible claim, since one of the first recorded images of a lady playing ice hockey is a picture of Isobel Preston, Lord Stanley's daughter, who was photographed playing hockey in 1890.

The first-ever newspaper account of a game between two women's teams appeared in the *Ottawa Citizen* on February 11, 1891. Although the teams were unnamed, it is still regarded as the first recorded game of women's ice hockey.

The Canadian Hockey Association says the first recorded women's hockey game took place in 1892 in Barrie, Ontario. Regardless, by the turn of the century, numerous women's hockey teams were playing all across Canada. Photos from the period indicate that the standard uniform included long wool skirts, turtleneck sweaters, hats and gloves.

By 1894, it was clear that the ladies were getting the hang of the game. College girls at McGill University in Montreal began playing weekly ice hockey games using male students to "guard" the door, while two teams of women ice hockey players were recorded playing a game on the artificial ice surface in Philadelphia's Ice Palace Arena.

In 1896, the *Ottawa Citizen* filed this report concerning women and ice hockey: "Both teams played grandly and surprised hundreds of the sterner sex who went to the match expecting to see many ludicrous scenes and have many good laughs. Indeed, before they were there very long, their sympathies and admiration had gone out to the teams. The men became wildly enthusiastic."

Perhaps the greatest break-through in the history of women's hockey came on November 17, 1992, when the Nagano Organizing Committee and an IOC Coordination Commission announced that women's hockey would be an official medal sport at the 1998 Winter Games.

Female Flashes

Let's not forget these female pioneers

BELOW: Team Quebec captured the Esso Women's championship in 2002-03.

OPPOSITE TOP: Judy Diduck, captain of the Canadian Women's University champion Alberta Pandas.

OPPOSITE BOTTOM LEFT: Laura Campbell (left) of the Aurora Panthers in action against Peterborough.

OPPOSITE BOTTOM RIGHT: Women have been playing hockey at the University of New Hampshire for 25 years.

Albertine Lapansee

Albertine played for the Cornwall Vics all-women's team from 1915–917, leading the club to the championship while accounting for 80 percent of her club's goals. Three years later, "she" was a "he" named Albert Smith following a sex-change operation in New York City, one of the first of its kind ever performed in North America.

Karen Koch

Although she had played goal for a Northern Michigan University fraternity team, she wasn't allowed to play for a Senior A men's club in Michigan.

Jane Yearwood

In 1970, she played goal for a boy's team in Edmonton, Alberta, without a mask!

Gail Cummings

Played four games with the Huntsville Minor Hockey Association All-Star team before being notified by Coach Barry Webb that her Canadian Amateur Hockey Association player registration certificate had been rejected.

Barbara Brody

A high-school senior in Oyster Bay, Long Island, New York, she won a discrimination suit against the town and was officially allowed to play "with the boys" in the town's high-school ice hockey league.

Danielle Dube

On December 11, 2002, Danielle Dube became only the third female to start a game in goal in a professional minor league game. Dube took the loss as the WCHL's San Diego Gulls dropped a 4-1 decision to the Long Beach Ice Dogs.

CHAPTER 2

THE HISTORY

T his section will dictate the history of the game of hockey, not through an examination of the rules or following a standard timeline, but through an account of the leagues, teams, equipment, arenas and front-office and back room architects that help make the game what is today.

The tapestry of the game can be found on the walls of the grand old barns that housed the game from it's earliest inception in 1875. Any old-timer who saw hockey played in the old-fashioned skating rinks that hosted the sport at the turn of the century would recognize the multiplex palaces where the games are played today.

We'll look at the various teams and leagues that have helped mold the game, from the first professional loop that was formed in Pittsburgh to some of the more obscure loops such as the All-Black league and unusual teams like the Windsor Swastikas.

The history of the game is also told by examining the weird and wonderful characters who have added flair and humor to the dressing rooms and the ice surfaces. The antics of such lovable lunatics as the Carlson brothers, Steve Durbano and Howie Young and the eccentricities of Eric Nesterenko, Roger Neilson and Harold Ballard all reveal as much about the history of the game as the record books.

No reflection on the game and its rich past would be complete without a quick peek into the zany minds of the owners, that brainy band of brothers who pulled the financial strings in the front office and pulled the wool over the players' eyes in the dressing room. Come on in. They're all here.

OPPOSITE: Pavel Bure, known as The Russian Rocket to his legion of fans, became the first Russian-trained sharpshooter to reach the 50-goal plateau in three different seasons. **BELOW RIGHT:** Eddie "The Entertainer" Shack (right) was the first NHL player to record a 20-goal season with five different teams. Sitting silently beside the motor-mouthed Shack is Frank "The Big M" Mahovlich, who became the first member of the Hockey Hall of Fame to be appointed to the Canadian Senate in 1998.

Teams and Leagues

First professional hockey league
Can't Blame Ya if You Didn't Say Pennsylvania

1902

ABOVE: The 1906 Pittsburgh Hockey Club, a charter member of the International Professional Hockey League, had future Hall-of-Fame members on its roster — Jimmy Gardner (back row, far left) and Tommy Smith (front row, far left).

ABOVE RIGHT: Jack "Doc" Gibson was instrumental in forming the International Professional Hockey League.

According to most hockey historians, the first fully professional hockey league in the history of the game was the International (Professional) Hockey League, a five-team loop based in Northern Michigan that began play in 1904. However, it took a hockey hound by the name of Ernie Fitzsimmons to sniff out the real truth.

The first pro league was the Western Pennsylvania Hockey League, which began play as an amateur loop in the late 1890s before becoming a fully paid, fully professional organization prior to the 1902–03 season. The league had four franchises that were based entirely in Pittsburgh, which had one of the best artificial ice surfaces in the world. The WPHL didn't have the "star" names that the IHL was able to recruit when it was the top pro loop, but it had its share of stars, one of whom was goaltender Riley Hern, who backstopped his way into the Hockey Hall of Fame in 1962. The professional version of the WPHL flourished for only two seasons before folding its tent in 1904 and taking a sabbatical until 1907. Ironically, the WPHL was resurrected to replace the IHL, which grew too fast and died too young.

First hockey team to disappear without a trace
Here We Are, Gone

1963

BELOW: A schedule from the CHL's 1976-77 season and a program for the CHL's forgotten team, the 1963-64 Indianapolis Caps. RIGHT: Indy Caps coach Pete Leswick humors goalie Hank Bassen.

The Indianapolis Capitols were one of the founding members of the newly formed Central Professional Hockey League that began play in 1963. Honest. As they say, you could look it up! On second thought, you'd better not. Even the league itself didn't acknowledge that the team existed.

The Capitols played nine games during that season before they were relocated to Cincinnati on November 7, 1963. They didn't want to leave Indianapolis, but tragedy, greed, circumstances and confusion led to their demise. On October 31, 1963, there was a horrific explosion at the Indianapolis Fairgrounds Coliseum, which was home to the newly anointed CHL franchise. During an Ice Follies show, an explosion demolished a large portion of the seating section, killing 74 people and injuring more than 400 others.

The incident occurred when propane, which was being used to keep the pre-popped popcorn warm, began leaking from a faulty valve. At 11:04 PM, the Coliseum was rocked by the first of two massive explosions that sent chunks of concrete flying through the air and created a huge fireball that critically injured a number of the patrons attending the ice show.

This left the Capitols without a home, but most of the Indianapolis hockey enthusiasts believed that as soon as the Coliseum was repaired, the team would return. But the Detroit Red Wings, who sponsored the club, were disappointed in the attendance at the arena and the performance of the team. Indy's lone home ice victory was a forfeit. So, the Motown brass decided to move the club permanently to Cincinnati.

The Coliseum was restored and is still used today. Renamed the Pepsi Coliseum in 1991, it is now the home of the CHL's Indianapolis Ice.

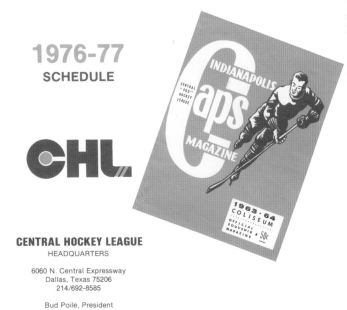

			SCORE	SCORE	
209.			SLC	at	KC
210.	Fri.	Mar. 25	FTW	at	OKC
211.			KC	at	SLC
212.			DAL	at	TUL
213.	Sat.	Mar. 26	DAL	at	FTW
214.			KC	at	SLC
215.			OKC	at	TUL
216.	Sun.	Mar. 27	OKC	at	DAL
217.			FTW	at	KC
218.	Mon.	Mar. 28	TUL	at	SLC
219.	Wed.	Mar. 30	OKC	at	FTW
220.			DAL	at	KC
221.			TUL	at	SLC
222.	Fri.	Apr. 1	KC	at	OKC
223.			DAL	at	SLC
224.			FTW	at	TUL
225.	Sat.	Apr. 2	TUL	at	DAL
226.			KC	at	FTW
227.			SLC	at	OKC
228.	Sun.	Apr. 3	FTW	at	DAL

1976-77 SCHEDULE

STARTING TIME OF
CENTRAL HOCKEY LEAGUE GAMES:

Salt Lake City—Mountain Time
All Others—Central Time

DALLAS BLACK HAWKS
All Games.................................... 7:30 p.m.

FT. WORTH TEXANS
All Games.................................... 7:30 p.m.

KANSAS CITY BLUES
All Games.................................... 7:30 p.m.

OKLAHOMA CITY BLAZERS
All Games.................................... 7:30 p.m.
Sundays .... 7:00 p.m.

SALT LAKE CITY GOLDEN EAGLES
All Games.................................... 7:30 p.m.

TULSA OILERS
All Games.................................... 7:30 p.m.

CENTRAL HOCKEY LEAGUE
HEADQUARTERS

6060 N. Central Expressway
Dallas, Texas 75206
214/692-8585

Bud Poile, President

First American pro team to play the Russians
Red Surge

1974

When teams from the Soviet Union toured North America during the 1960s, they insisted they play only against other "amateur" teams like themselves.

However, after the "Series of the Century" between a team of NHL pros and the Soviet National Team in September of 1972, the rules of combat were dramatically altered. The Soviets may have lost the eight-game series by a whisker, but they learned a valuable lesson about capitalism: it was paid in cold, hard American currency. So, it wasn't surprising that the Russians were more than willing to tour the USA again and take on all comers.

On January 5, 1974, the Seattle Totems of the Western Hockey League, a minor league loop with a rich history, became the first American-based team to square off against the Big Red Machine. With more than 12,000 fevered fans cheering on their heroes, the Totems attacked the Russians from the opening face-off, winning key battles in the corners and matching the Soviets goal for goal.

The Reds were surprised by the tenacity and skills of the minor-league pros and struggled through the first 30 minutes. But like a hawk on the prowl, once the Soviets sensed the Seattle club was running out of gas, they pounced on their prey. With the score tied 4-4, the Russians blitzed the Totem defense, slamming home five consecutive goals — including a three-goal effort by Alexander Yakushev — before departing the Pacific Northwest with a convincing 9-4 victory.

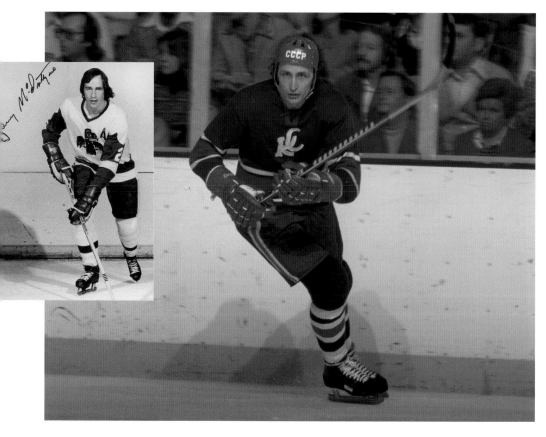

First team to have a "curse" placed on them

Did He Fall or Was He Pushed?

1927

t's not every day that a professional sports franchise team
has a curse put on them. It's even odder when the supposed
"curse" actually seemed to take effect! When Pete Muldoon
was supposedly gassed as the Black Hawks coach following
the 1926–27 season, he stormed into the offices of owner
Major McLaughlin and told his former boss, "If you fire me,
Major, you'll never finish first! I'll put a curse on this team that
will hoodoo it till the end of time!"

And for many years it appeared that curse was taking
effect. Although the club did win a trio of Stanley Cup titles,
they never finished on the top rung of the regular season standings until the 1966–67 season. And even then, despite superstar
talent like Hull, Mikita, Hall, Esposito, Pilote, Wharram and Vasko,
the Hawks were booted out of the playoffs by the Toronto
Maple Leafs, who finished 19 points behind the Hawks. That
collapse prompted Toronto sportswriter Jim Coleman to admit he
had conjured up the whole scheme 25 years earlier in a story he
wrote about the struggling franchise in 1943. Muldoon actually
resigned on March 17, 1927, but agreed to handle coaching duties
through to the end of the season.

First team to score five empty net goals in one game

Open (Net) Season

1970

The Chicago Black Hawks secured their place in the history of hockey oddities when they scored five empty net goals in a single game. By doing so, the Hawks altered the course of hockey history during the 1970s.

The game in question was a Chicago/Montreal match on April 5, 1970, the final date on the NHL's 1969–70 schedule. It also featured the defending Stanley Cup champion Montreal Canadiens engaging themselves in an almost suicidal game of Russian roulette in a desperate attempt to make the playoffs. The Habs entered the final game of the season two points up on the NY Rangers. By demolishing the Red Wings 9-5 in an afternoon match, the Broadway Blueshirts tied the Habs in the standings, but held the playoff trump card because they had scored four more goals than the Habs over the course of the season. The Habs knew a win or a fistful of goals would put them into the playoff parade.

By the midway point of the third period, the Habs were losing 5-2. So, Montreal coach Claude Ruel pulled the goalie Rogie Vachon with 10:44 left to play, in a vain attempt to score the necessary goals to upset the Rangers' post-season party plans.

The Habs were unable to solve the steady goaltending of Tony Esposito, but the Hawks had a field day, filling the vacated Montreal net with rubber. In the final nine minutes of the game, the Hawks slipped five pucks into the empty Canadiens' net, establishing a record that will never be matched.

The following season, the Black Hawks were moved from the East Division to the West, where they feasted on the weaker opposition until the ascent of the Philadelphia Flyers. The League also clarified its tie-breaking rules, giving the results of the head-to-head confrontations between the tied teams greater weight than the total goals scored over the course of a season.

First team to wear a swastika on the uniform

It Is Not What You Think

1905-1916

During the 2002 Christmas season, some alarming news splashed over the airwaves concerning toys adorned with swastikas that were found in traditional Christmas snap-and-pull crackers. Historians tried to point out that the swastika was an ancient symbol that was not representative of Nazi Germany or the dictatorial regime that sparked World War II.

For the record, there was a hockey team who wore the swastika in an age when it was still a symbol of peace, luck and fortune.

The team in question was the Windsor Swastikas, a hockey club formed in Nova Scotia in the early 1900s. The team traveled throughout the Maritime Provinces, even voyaging as far as St. John's, Newfoundland, for hockey matches. To the fine folks in Windsor, the team that proudly displayed the symbol on their jerseys was a high-scoring, top-notch club that represented the community.

The crimes that were perpetrated from 1932 to 1944 have forever tarnished the swastika, but some historians believe the four interlocking "L's" meant Love, Life, Luck and Light. Others interpreted it as crossed lightning bolts symbolizing a source of great power. To the Romans, the swastika meant "Peace." To the Hindus, it meant "Good Fortune" and to the American Plains Indians, it simply meant "Good Luck."

Ice Houses, Old Barns, and Rinks of Renown

The first "hockey" rink

No Intentions in the Dimensions

1863

ABOVE: Victoria Rink, built in 1862 and closed in 1937, was home to the first organized hockey match played according to a written set of rules and featuring uniformed teams.

The world's first covered rink was built in Quebec City in 1852, but it wasn't until ten years later that the world's first "famous" arena was erected. Dubbed the Victoria Skating Rink and located at the intersection of Stanley and Drummond Streets in Montreal, this marvelous ice palace was opened in 1863 and remained open until 1937. Although this and most of the other early rinks were intended for skating, not for ice hockey, the Victoria rink's ice surface (202' x 85') provided the guidelines for what would eventually become the standard size of a hockey rink. On March 3, 1875, the rink played host to what is now universally recognized as the first organized hockey match.

On July 2, 2002, Rene Fasel, the president of the International Ice Hockey Federation (IIHF), announced that the Victoria Skating Rink was officially being recognized as "the cradle of hockey." Fasel wrote, "The site of the game can be precisely identified. The game was played on a confined area called a rink with a size (202 feet by 85 feet), which basically defined the game as we know it today. Not many sports can, as precisely as hockey, identify the origins of its game. This is of great historical value to us."

First artificial ice rink
Baby, It's Cold Inside!

1876

W hile England deserves credit for opening the first artificial ice arena, an American was the first to forge the idea. On November 1, 1870, Matthew Bujac was awarded the rights to US patent # 108868, which contained the plans necessary to build the world's first artificial ice-making machine. Bujac and investor William Newton attempted to erect an arena in New York City to test the invention, but the facility never opened.

The first refrigerated ice surface in England opened in Charing Cross, London, in 1876. Designed by a Professor Gamgee, the rink had a 100-square-foot surface constructed over a network of copper pipes. A mixture of glycerin and water was circulated through the tubes after they had been chilled by ether. The pipes were then covered with water and a coating of ice formed over the pipes.

Canada was a distant trailer in the construction of arenas that were capable of generating ice mechanically. It was not until 1911 that the first artificial ice rinks were built. Designed and constructed by Lester and Frank Patrick, rinks were opened in both Vancouver and Victoria, in British Columbia. The following year, the first artificial ice rink in Eastern Canada was built in Toronto. But progress was slow. In 1920, there were still only four artificial ice rinks in the entire country.

First arena to have unbreakable glass
Windex, Anyone?

1947

ABOVE: Rocket Richard shatters the unbreakable Plexiglas myth. Maple Leaf Gardens was also the first NHL facility to have a state-of-the-art score clock that hung from the rafters above center ice and the first rink to have escalators carry patrons to the upper levels of the arena.
RIGHT: Bill "The Fireman" Juzda was the human propellant who sent the Rocket soaring.

The first NHL arena to replace the wire fencing that was commonly used to protect fans was Toronto's Maple Leaf Gardens. Installed shortly after the Christmas break during the 1946–47 season, the usual "wire fencing" that surrounded the end zones of the rink was replaced by a series of clear panes of what appeared to be glass.

The new material protecting fans from soaring pucks, flying sticks, and hurling players was called Herculite or Plexiglas, a thermoplastic synthetic resin invented at McGill University in Montreal by research student William Chalmers in 1930.

The main claim that made Herculite glass unique was that it was supposedly unbreakable. On December 14, 1949, that theory was put to the test and laid to rest. Late in the first period of the game between the Leafs and the Montreal Canadiens, Rocket Richard was drilled skates-first into the glass. Richard struck the glass at such an angle that the pane exploded into a shower of minute pieces.

Referee George Gravel sent the teams to their dressing rooms and tacked the remaining time onto the start of the second stanza. Five fans were treated for cuts and bruises, but none of the injuries was considered serious.

The official photographers for the Toronto Maple Leafs at the time were Nat and Lou Turofsky, and they captured the exact moment that Richard's skate shattered the glass, creating one of the most famous images in the history of the game.

The photo that appeared in the newspapers the following day showed the incredible scene. However, the picture was cropped and showed only Richard falling to the ice as Toronto forward Cal Gardner watched in amazement. Since Gardner is the only other player in the frame, most pundits assumed he was the Leaf who launched the Rocket into the stratosphere. However, the true full-frame image tells the true story. It was Bill Juzda, the ferocious fireman from Winnipeg and one of the Richard's most hated rivals, who rocked the Rocket and helped create one of the finest moments in the history of photojournalism.

First arena to feature octopus tossing

An Olympia Sport

1952

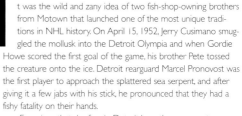

BELOW TOP: When it's playoff time in Hockeytown, USA, the octopus becomes an integral part of the Stanley Cup tradition. **BOTTOM:** A linesman uses a borrowed stick to remove this unwelcome eight-armed guest that found its way onto the ice surface at the "Joe."

t was the wild and zany idea of two fish-shop-owning brothers from Motown that launched one of the most unique traditions in NHL history. On April 15, 1952, Jerry Cusimano smuggled the mollusk into the Detroit Olympia and when Gordie Howe scored the first goal of the game, his brother Pete tossed the creature onto the ice. Detroit rearguard Marcel Pronovost was the first player to approach the splattered sea serpent, and after giving it a few jabs with his stick, he pronounced that they had a fishy fatality on their hands.

Ever since that day, fans in Detroit have thrown an octopus or dozen onto the ice during every Red Wings playoff appearance. However, after the plastic rat infestation that constantly interrupted play during the 1996 Florida Panthers playoff run, the league outlawed all "ritual" littering of the ice with the exception of tossing hats to celebrate a three-goal performance.

The new rule only postponed the octopus parade. Come playoff time in the Motor City, some fan will always find a clandestine way to toss an octopus onto the ice during the Red Wings' post-season search for Lord Stanley's silverware.

First arena to feature rat tossing
Rats Patrol

1995

BELOW TOP: One of the fine furry friends on the ice during the Panthers' playoff run in 1995.
BOTTOM: "I spend ten years in this league, work hard every night, get my share of goals, and now I'm going to go down in history as Rat Man."— Scott Mellanby's take on his dubious claim to fame.

Prior to the Florida Panthers home opener against Calgary in 1995, Panthers captain Scott Mellanby spied a rat casually parading through the team's dressing room at the Miami Arena in Fort Lauderdale. With the eye of an artist and the aim of a sniper, Mellanby speared his stick towards the offending rodent and nailed the beast with a single shot.

After he went out and scored a pair of goals that evening, the media embellished the tale by claiming that Mellanby had recorded the first "Rat Trick" in league history. From that moment on, Panthers fans showered the ice with plastic rats whenever the Panthers scored an important goal. The ploy worked like magic and the Panthers became the first expansion team to reach the Stanley finals in their first five years of operation since the league realigned in 1970.

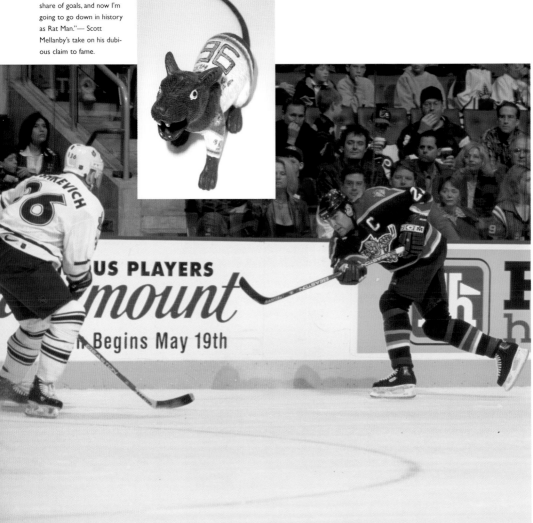

First arena to feature towel tossing
Raising the White Flag

1982

ABOVE: The Vancouver Canucks may have sketched the idea, but it was the Winnipeg Jets who painted the masterpiece. When the team requested fans wear white for the opening game of the 1985 playoffs, the Jets' faithful responded by turning the Winnipeg Arena into a sea of white shirts, jerseys and towels. The whiteout was born.

In the 1982 playoffs, the Vancouver Canucks were immersed in a tough "winner take all" struggle with the Chicago Black Hawks to determine which Western Conference club would be fed to the awaiting Stanley Cup defending sharks from Long Island.

In the second game of the Hawks-Canucks series, the ice seemed oddly tilted in the Black Hawks' favor. The referee charged the Canucks with nine rule infractions that required sin-bin time and even disallowed one of the Canucks' goals.

Coach Neilson viewed the on-ice chaos as a blatant case of favoritism. In protest, he draped a white towel over the end of a hockey stick and proceeded to "wave the white flag of surrender."

When the Canucks returned to Vancouver for the next game, thousands of fans greeted the team by waving white towels in recognition of their coach's protest. Neilson's spontaneous "gesture" has since become a tradition followed by sports fans of all sports throughout North America.

First ice hockey arena to host a championship football game

'Da Bears

1932

BELOW: This skeleton of twisted steal, once Chicago Stadium, lovingly known as "The Madhouse on Madison" because of its boisterous beer-bellied fans and booming pipe organ, fell victim to the wrecking ball in 1995.

n 1932, the Portsmouth Spartans and the Chicago Bears finished the NFL season in a tie for first place with identical 6-1-4 records, an oddity that had never occurred in the history of the league. So, for the first time, both teams agreed to play a one-game "winner take all" playoff match on December 18th in Chicago. By game day, the Chicago area was in the grip of a severe winter storm that blanketed the city with waist-deep snow and sub-zero temperatures. After prolonged debate, the championship game was moved to Chicago Stadium, home of the NHL Black Hawks. The circus was slated to come to the Windy City the following week and the floor of the arena was already covered with dirt. After a few rule modifications — the indoor game was on. The hometown Bears shut-out the Spartans by a 9-0 score and captured the NFL title.

First arena to cancel a game because of a speech
State of the Union

2001

When George W. Bush speaks, people listen, even hockey players. As the U.S. president was preparing to address a joint session of Congress and the American public on September 20, 2001, the Philadelphia Flyers and the New York Rangers were in the middle of an entertaining, hard-fought exhibition tussle that was deadlocked at two goals apiece. When the president's thirty-six-minute speech began, the game was momentarily halted so both the spectators and the players could watch and hear the president's message on the giant screen above center ice. Coming on the heels of the tragedy that hit the USA on September 11th, the president's message was a much-needed remedy for a nation in need of consoling.

When the P.A. announcer informed the sold-out gathering at the Fleet Center that the game was about to resume, the fans demanded that the president's speech be played in its entirety by booing and chanting "Leave it on! Leave it on!"

So the arena brass had no choice but to accept the edict of the fans. The crowd, players, and referees sat and listened to the president's poignant words. When the speech was concluded, the cheering in the rink eclipsed the applause in the House of Representatives.

After the speech, the officials and the players decided to line up, shake hands and declare the game a 2-2 tie. Not a single fan complained.

It wasn't the first time that a game was interrupted by a State of the Union address, however. On December 9, 1941, a game between Chicago and Boston was delayed for nearly half an hour as the 10,000 fans who were present listened to President Franklin D. Roosevelt declare that America was at war.

Arena anecdotes
Rink Raps

BELOW TOP: An "old-fashioned" game of hoops on skates entertained fans in between periods of the NY Americans-Chicago game on February 1, 1940. BOTTOM: Over 74,000 raving fans watched the Wolverines attack the Spartans on a specially designed piece of frozen tundra.

First covered arena in Canada
On March 1, 1863, the first covered skating rink in Canada opened in Halifax, Nova Scotia.

First arena to have separate penalty boxes
Believe it or not, it wasn't until November 8, 1963, that Maple Leaf Gardens became the first arena to install separate penalty boxes. Prior to this historic date, players from both sides shared the same sin-bin.

First NHL arena to use a Zamboni
On March 10, 1955, the Montreal Forum became the first NHL arena to use a Zamboni to clean the ice surface between periods.

First arena to have 75,000 fans watch a hockey game
On October 7, 2001, the Michigan State Spartans and the University of Michigan Wolverines battled to a 3-3 draw in front of 74,554 fans at Michigan State's Spartan Stadium. That eclipsed the previous top draw of 55,000 fans who had gathered at Lenin Stadium in Moscow to watch the 1957 World Championship game between Sweden and the Soviet Union.

ABOVE: Spartan Stadium became the world's largest ice hockey arena on October 7, 2001.
RIGHT: A lone hockey net shines majestically in the twilight's last gleaming.

The Weird, the Wild and the Wonderful

First player to win a Stanley Cup, Canadian Football and Canadian Boxing Title

A Jack of All Trades and the Master of Them All

1898, 1899 1900, 1903-06

BELOW: Harvey Pulford during his glory days with the Ottawa Hockey Club. Pulford may have set the pace, but Lionel Conacher won the race. In addition to his Hall of Fame prowess on the ice, Conacher was a AAA batting champion, won the Grey Cup in football, compiled a 27-0 record as a pro wrestler, captured the Canadian light-heavyweight boxing title and still had time to play professional lacrosse.

His name isn't instantly recognizable, but among the sporting elite in the early half of the 20th century, there was no athlete finer than Harvey Pulford. A member of the dynamic Ottawa Silver Seven, Pulford captained the club to the Stanley Cup championship in three consecutive years, from 1903 to 1906, defeating ten different challengers along the way.

When he wasn't winning ice hockey trophies, Pulford could be found on the gridiron as a member of the Ottawa football team that won Canadian football titles in 1898, 1899, and 1900. Since he was handy with a hockey stick, Harv figured he would be adept with a lacrosse stick and became a key member of the Ottawa Capitals lacrosse team that was the cream of the crop during the last four years of the 19th century. In the square circle, Pulford showed he had a keen knowledge of the "sweet science," capturing both the Eastern Canada light-heavyweight and heavyweight boxing titles. Pulford's exploits weren't confined to dry land, however. He was just as competitive — and successful — on the water, winning numerous International honors in paddling and rowing. Throw in his Ottawa championship in the sport of squash in 1922–23, and you have the resume of a remarkable athlete.

First player to have his hairpiece stolen during a game

This Lid's for You

1978

With his bronzed tan, 15" biceps and muscle-beach physique, Bobby Hull was the NHL's first poster boy. Nicknamed the "Golden Jet" because of his golden locks and sensational speed, Hull was super-sensitive about his hair, especially when he started to lose it. It was then that Hull decided to become one of the first hockey players to sport a toupee. Yes, Hull wore a rug.

Of course, Hull's opponents were aware of his false lid, but there wasn't a player crazy enough to mess with it—until Steve Durbano showed up.

A troubled, but talented player, Durbano was a first-round draft pick of the New York Rangers in 1971. His willingness to engage in fisticuffs at anytime, both on and off the ice, earned Durbano the nickname "Demolition Durby."

It was on April 14, 1978, during a playoff game between the Winnipeg Jets and Birmingham Bulls in the WHA, that "Demo Durby" decided to go where no player had ever dared go before. Midway through the match, a melee broke out and, as usual, Durbano was in the middle of the fracas. While various combatants were locked in a loveless embrace, Durbano skated up to Hull and ripped the rug from his head. What happened next is one of those glorious moments that everyone remembers, though no two stories are the same. Depending on who is telling the tale, Durbano tossed it, ripped it, ate it or shot it.

Everyone has an opinion on what happened, including Dave Hanson, who played one of the infamous Hanson Brothers in the movie *Slapshot*. Since he was actually a member of the Birmingham team at the time, even Hanson has staked a claim as the player responsible for yanking Hull's hair. One thing we do know for certain is that the Golden Jet left the ice and returned wearing a helmet — to hide both his shining bulb and his embarrassment.

First doctor to play on
a Stanley Cup-winning team

Medic!

1922

BELOW TOP: Rod Smylie
was a multi-talented athlete
who held the Canadian
record for the 440-yard
dash during his years as
a student at the University
of Toronto.
BOTTOM: The Stanley
Cup-winning Toronto St.
Pats, who captured Lord
Stanley's silver chalice in
1922.
OPPOSITE: Dr. Randy
Gregg celebrates his fifth
Stanley Cup victory after
the Oilers downed the
Boston Bruins in the 1990
Finals.

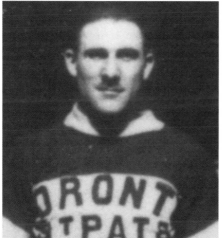

Unless the history books are playing tricks on us, it's safe to assume that Rod Smylie was the first certified medical doctor to be a member of a Stanley Cup-winning team. Smylie proved to be just as talented with blades on his feet as he was with scalpels in his hands, helping the Toronto Dentals club capture the Allan Cup in 1917.

In 1920, Smylie signed with the NHL's Toronto St. Pats and began a career of balancing responsibilities in the hospital with his duties on the ice. When the St. Pats defeated the Vancouver Millionaires to win the Stanley Cup in 1922, Dr. Smylie became the first M.D. to have his name inscribed on Lord Stanley's silver mug.

Almost six decades later, another young medical student made his mark in the NHL. After starting his professional hockey career in Japan while completing medical school, Randy Gregg returned to Canada and was signed by the Edmonton Oilers. Dr. Gregg went on to become a fixture on the Oilers' blueline and a member of four Stanley Cup-winning teams.

NHL "weekends only" player

Mixing Brains with Brawn

1956

BELOW: "I'm just not interested in the power of money, but that's the way the score is kept, by the amount of money you earn." — Eric Nesterenko
BOTTOM: Eric Nesterenko (15) runs interference on Toronto's Red Kelly during the 1962 Stanley Cup finals. Another player who mixed academia with athletics was Gordon Roberts, who played with the Montreal Wanderers from 1911 to 1916 while earning his degree in medicine at McGill University.

When Eric Nesterenko joined the Toronto Maple Leafs in 1953, he came with a reputation as a player who marched to his own drummer. He also carried the added weight of being called "the next Jean Beliveau."

Despite his promising credentials, size and ability, Nesterenko failed to deliver the goods on the ice. He was shredded by the press so often that he concluded it would be in his best interests to retire and return to university to continue his studies. In an interview at the time, Nesterenko proved he wasn't quite "like" the other athletes who played the game. "I have doubts about what I do," he once admitted, "I'm not that sure of myself. It doesn't seem clear to me at times. I'm a man playing at a boy's game. Is this a valid reason for making money?"

When the Leafs realized Nesterenko was serious about abandoning the game, they sold his rights to the Chicago Black Hawks. Nesterenko had no intention of returning to the NHL, but Chicago made him an offer he couldn't refuse. The Hawks agreed to allow him to play on a part-time basis while attending university. As a result, Nesterenko played only the weekends during the 1956–57 campaign. Slowly, Nesterenko rediscovered his passion for the game and he continued to play competitive hockey until the mid-1970s.

While Nesterenko's situation was odd, it wasn't unique. During the 1942–43 season, Frank "Judge" Dunlop played only home games, which were invariably on the weekends, for both the St. Michael's Majors and the Toronto Maple Leafs. During the week, the Judge could usually be found cramming in the University of Toronto library, studying to pass his bar exam.

First player to come back from the dead

Hey, Hey, Up He Rises

2002

Many athletes have "come back from the dead" in terms of resurrecting their careers, but few can match the miraculous comeback of Ross Knipfel. Shortly after enlisting in the Canadian Army, Knipfel reported to the medic to receive his Army-regulated anti-epidemic injection before shipping out and heading overseas. After the doctor had administered the shots, the young defenseman suddenly collapsed. Upon examination, it was discovered that he was in a state of cardiac arrest. A dose of adrenaline was administered to the comatose private and a full two minutes passed before he was revived. The Army reasoned that if the big blond blue-liner couldn't take a simple injection, it was doubtful he could take the strain of warfare. So, Knipfel was discharged and went on to play with Providence, Pittsburgh and Buffalo in the AHL.

This story bears an eerie resemblance to a recent event that occurred during a Western Hockey League game between Spokane and Calgary on November 22, 2002. Late in the second period of a 2-2 tie, Spokane defenseman Darren Lefebvre collapsed shortly after finishing a shift. The stricken player was removed from the Chiefs' bench, where the team doctors discovered they couldn't detect a pulse. When CPR failed, a defibrillator was tried and it took three shocks from the paddles to revive the young man's heart. Doctors estimate it may have been as long as 20 minutes before Lefebvre's ticker finally began to keep time. While there was some damage detected near the bottom of Lefebvre's heart, it is a problem that can be solved with medication. Like Knipfel before him, Lefebvre had made a remarkable return from the dead.

First lacrosse goal
Getting a Legg Up

1996

ABOVE: Mike Legg (#15) scores a goal the "conventional" way during his exceptional career with the University of Michigan. Legg's infamous "lacrosse" goal against the University of Minnesota was one of the three finalists for ESPN's Play of the Year in 1996.

B ill Morrison, a career minor-leaguer who ran a top-notch hockey school during the off-season, had one particular stunt he used to arouse the attention of his pupils and instructors. Armstrong would scoop up the puck with the blade of his stick, cradle the puck in the crease of the curve and whip it, lacrosse-style, towards the net. It was a great trick and always created roars of laughter.

One employee at that summer camp was a young collegian named Mike Legg who attended the University of Michigan. In the 1996 NCAA West Regional Quarterfinals, Michigan was trailing the University of Minnesota Golden Gophers by a slim 2-1 score. In the opening minutes of the second period, Legg found himself behind the Gopher cage, with a loose puck at his feet and a clear lane around the net. In a moment of artistic brilliance, Legg scooped up the idle disc just as Armstrong had illustrated and sneaked around the side of the Gopher crease before tucking the tying goal under the crossbar. The bewildered pose of netminder Steve DuBus, who was left dumbfounded in the Minnesota net, is one of the great sporting images of all time. Legg's goal was featured in *Sports Illustrated* and earned the ultimate accolade when it was deemed to be CNN's "Play of the Day."

First owner to sign himself to a pro contract

It's My Party and I'll Skate If I Want To!

1990-91

I n 1990, the Albany Choppers were granted admission into the International Hockey League under the ownership of David Welker, who was a former owner of the Fort Wayne Komets. Welker signed a sponsorship deal with the Price Chopper supermarket chain and dubbed his new franchise the Choppers. Welker even signed himself to a player's contract, which guaranteed him $11,000 for the year and health insurance coverage through the Players' Union.

The Choppers were a miserable mess, both on and off the ice. Players were swapped like hockey cards, fans stayed away in droves and there was little or no money to pay the players. In fact, there wasn't even enough cash in the company coffers to purchase new sticks. This led to one of the more comedic chapters of an otherwise dismal season.

On January 31, 1991, the Choppers defeated the Fort Wayne Komets in a double-overtime shootout when Jim McGeough scored the winning goal. McGeough wasn't exactly known for his offensive skills, so it seemed odd that he was the player chosen to take such an important shot. "The only reason he won it," explained coach Dave Allison, "was because he had a good stick. It was basically the only good stick we had."

By the time Valentine's Day rolled around, there wasn't any money available for the next road trip and there was certainly no cash on hand to pay the players. And so it was that the Albany Choppers had their hearts broken, their doors locked and their franchise taken away.

81

First ordained minister to play goalie in the NHL
In God, We Trust

1943

BELOW: Art Ross was not only one of the finest rearguards to play the game, he was also one of hockey's greatest architects. Ross designed the modern goal net which is still used today; introduced the smooth-edged or "beveled" puck to the sport; initiated the first system for compiling "plus/minus" statistics; and served as a NHL referee, coach and general manager for over 30 years.

During World War II, a majority of NHL players were either overseas in the Armed Services, or stationed at army bases throughout Canada and the United States. Their absence from the on-ice wars created a number of "job" openings for players who would never have had the opportunity to play in the NHL otherwise.

One of those lucky lads was a man of the cloth named George Abbott. Pastor Abbott, an ordained minister with the Soldiers and Army Christian Association, also served as the Toronto Maple Leafs practice goaltender. Another of his responsibilities was serving as the emergency goaltender during Leafs games at the Gardens.

On November 27, 1943, the Boston Bruins found themselves without a cage cop when incumbent netminder Bert Gardiner became ill. Abbott was commissioned to take Gardiner's place, stopping 46 of 53 shots as the Leafs bumped off the Bruins by a count of 7-4.

Abbott was pleased with both his performance and the excellent outing by his employers. "I think the Leafs played as well as they've ever played this winter," Abbott told the press, "and it had to be against me." Boston general manager Art Ross was less than complimentary. "Don't ask me about him," he snarled, "All I know is that it was either a question of playing goal myself or getting a substitute. And I wound up with this fellow."

First bat to interrupt a playoff game

A Laureate for Lorentz

1975

Somehow bats and hockey just seem to go together. Both perform best at night, operate on instinct and become nasty and temperamental when angry.

So, it's only natural that a bat was the first creepy critter to interrupt a Stanley Cup playoff game. And it picked a very appropriate evening to make its presence felt. The date was May 20, 1975, the place was the Buffalo Auditorium, the teams were the Buffalo Sabres and Philadelphia Flyers and the temperature inside the Aud was 118 degrees.

Since there was no air conditioning in the building, the arena became congested with fog, forcing the players to skate around the ice, waving towels and sheets in an attempt to clear the air. Suddenly, from out of a smoky mist came a bat, which began to navigate its way towards the ice surface. Buffalo sniper Jim Lorentz spied the culprit and with one deft swipe of his stick, downed the enemy flier. Only Rick MacLeish of the Flyers had the nerve to approach the now dormant nocturnal mammal. He picked it up with the blade of his stick and deposited the beast in the only place it belonged — the penalty box.

First deaf hockey player
Are You Receiving Me?

1983

OPPOSITE: The first
legally deaf player to make
it to the NHL, Jim Kyte was
often forced to let his fists
do the talking for him. A
tireless combatant who
played a clean, hard-nosed
style, Kyte was a respected
opponent on the ice and an
admired citizen outside the
dressing room.
ABOVE: "When I played
Junior, one guy used to call
me 'Radio Shack' all the
time."— Jim Kyte.

When he finally made it to the NHL, hard-rock rear-guard Jim Kyte knew it was his hands that got him there and it was his hands that were going to keep him there. Kyte was known as a stay-at-home defenseman, a no-nonsense defender who guarded his goalie's crease by nailing any member of the opposition who dared infringe on his territory. And if a solid two-hander across the back or a swift chop to the ankle didn't remove the enemy skater, a quick uppercut and a few cuffs to the side of the head usually would.

But Kyte also needed his hands to sign. Not for autographs though. Kyte was legally deaf and needed his hands for sign language.

When he was playing, Kyte wore a pair of top-quality hearing aids to help him anticipate a hit by an incoming opponent and stay focused on the action around him. "I have the biggest problem with background noise," he admitted. "When I played in the old Chicago Stadium, it was very loud. I wouldn't hear the whistle and I'd be playing when everyone else had stopped."

Its been said that the loss of hearing or sight seems to amplify the reception in other senses. Well, Kyte may have been deaf, but he certainly heard the voice of the game he loved. As a hockey analyst with a weekly editorial column in the *Ottawa Citizen*, Kyte scripts poetic insights into the game, analyzing its faults and praising the features that make it such a terrific sport.

First hockey theme
to be played for 35 years
Anthem for a Nation

1968

BELOW: The Barenaked
Ladies belt out Canada's
"real" national anthem
before a packed house at
the Air Canada Center in
Toronto.

The most famous piece of hockey music ever written was actually composed by a woman who was a real hockey fan. A classically trained musician from Vancouver, Dolores Claman was making "ends meet" by composing commercial jingles when the Canadian Broadcasting Corporation commissioned her to write a piece of theme music for the opening credits of Hockey Night in Canada in 1968.

"What I had in mind was I was thinking about how great people feel when a goal is scored," she recalled "rather than something to march along with, which is what they used to have…something to raise your spirit, and it worked."

It worked? That's an understatement. It's the unofficial anthem of the nation located North of the 49th parallel.

First hockey player to become a porn star, NOT!

This Butler Didn't Do It

1982-83

ABOVE: Although he gained notoriety for being misidentified as an adult film star, Jerry Butler easily could have been mistaken for two other men who really do share his name. One is Jerry Butler, a wide receiver who spent seven seasons with the Buffalo Bills and the other is Jerry Butler, the smooth-singing crooner who helped create what later became known as the Philadelphia Sound in the 1970s.

n the 1980s, rumors were rampant that a former member of the NY Rangers and Toronto Maple Leafs was establishing himself as a "big" star in the adult movie business. The player — and actor — in question was Jerry Butler. But they are two different people.

The Jerry Butler who starred in such box office "smashes" as *Hush, My Mother Might Hear* and *Great Sexpectations* was not the same Jerry Butler who starred at Madison Square Garden. So how did such a case of mistaken identity occur?

When the Jerry Butler of "adult entertainment" fame was born, his name was actually Paul Seiderman. It seems Mr. Seiderman was also an accomplished hockey player who played so effectively at the college level, he was granted an invite to participate in a NY Rangers tryout camp with hundreds of other NHL wanna-be's.

Years later, a cub reporter for a New York area weekly discovered Seiderman's (also known as Butler's) name in a dusty file that listed all the players who at one time or another had been placed on the NY Ranger's negotiation list. We can only assume why the junior reporter recognized Seiderman's name, but he pursued the story long enough to link Seiderman with Butler. Well, that was enough to get the rumor wheel turning, which generated a lot of speculation and newspaper copy. Although he was wrong, the long-forgotten never let the facts interfere with the story.

Heroes On and Off the Ice

First hockey player
to die in an airplane crash
The Best There Ever Was

1918

BELOW: Hobey Baker
(center) was the corner-
stone of the prestigious
New York St. Nicholas
Hockey Club, a senior team
that still exists today. In
2003, they captured the
Hockey USA Elite Senior
championship for the
second consecutive season.

The first true American-born ice hockey star was Hobey Baker. Universally recognized as the greatest amateur hockey player ever developed in the United States, Baker thrilled spectators with his ability to weave his way through the opposition. At full speed Baker would bank a pass off the boards, leap out of the path of an oncoming defender by balancing himself atop the dasher boards and jump back onto the ice in time to retrieve his own pass and drill the puck past the unsuspecting netminder.

Baker was also a ferocious fighter pilot and squadron commander who served his country with valor and distinction in World War I. Perhaps it was those very skills that caused his death. Shortly after the conclusion of the conflict overseas, Baker volunteered to test a newly repaired aircraft before returning to the United States. The plane malfunctioned and Baker was killed when the aircraft crashed to the ground.

After graduating from Princeton, Baker moved to New York City and joined the esteemed St. Nicholas hockey team. An amateur club with a top-notch pedigree, the team barnstormed up and down the Eastern Seaboard. When the club pulled into a new town, they were often greeted with billboards proclaiming "Baker plays here tonight." Even the skeptical press in Montreal had to admit that, "Uncle Sam has the cheek to develop a first class hockey player who was not born in Montreal."

First Hall of Fame member to die in action during World War I

From the Bench to the Trench

1916

Frank McGee, the offensive dynamo who scored 14 goals in the Ottawa Silver Seven's 23-2 trouncing of the Dawson City Nuggets on January 16, 1905, was not supposed to be serving his country in World War I. He wasn't even supposed to be in the army.

Although he was the first superstar of the game, and scoring machine whose recorded brilliance in Stanley Cup play will never be matched, McGee was blind in one eye, the result of an errant stick striking his eye early in his career.

The army does not accept one-eyed soldiers into their ranks, but somehow McGee received permission from the doctors and suited up for his country. There are numerous theories as to how McGee fooled the doctors into believing he could see from both eyes including a "hand is the quicker than the eye" routine that involved a right hand/left hand over the same eye routine. Perhaps the actual truth is simply that McGee called in a marker. He was the nephew of Thomas D'Arcy McGee, the only political figure to be assassinated in Canadian history.

Regardless, McGee served his country with distinction before losing his life during the Battle of the Somme on September 16, 1916. He is the only member of the Hockey Hall of Fame to be killed defending his country and his flag.

First NHL player to win the Military Cross

Decorating Duncan

1918

BELOW: Art Duncan played pro hockey in Vancouver, Calgary, Detroit, Toronto and Windsor after returning from overseas. One Military Cross winner who didn't come home was Percival Molson, the captain of the McGill University team in 1902-03. The football stadium on the Montreal campus is named in his honor.

A member of the 228th Battalion hockey team that began the 1916–17 season in the National Hockey Association, Art Duncan was shipped overseas with the entire team in 1917, where he quickly rose to the rank of Captain in the Royal Flying Corps.

In July of 1918, Duncan attacked a regiment of German soldiers who were pinning down a group of Canadian infantrymen. Buzzing the enemy at an altitude of only 100 feet, he destroyed the opposition before soaring off to nail a couple of German fighter planes moving in to attack.

Duncan added to his list of military achievements in September of 1918. Spying a hostile gaggle of 15 enemy planes attacking eight Canadian flyers, Duncan joined the fray and shot down one plane and held off the others in a spirited display of "cat-and-mouse" until the Canadian planes could re-group. For good measure, Duncan followed an enemy Albatross to a height of 200 feet before blowing it out of the sky. On September 16, 1918, he was awarded the Military Cross.

When he returned to North America, he returned to his first love, the game of hockey. He played eight seasons in the PCHA, WCHL and WHL before signing on with the NHL's Detroit Cougars. He later spent five seasons with the Toronto Maple Leafs, eventually becoming the bench boss of the club in 1931.

First NHL player to die in World War II
Dudley Did Right

1944

Dudley "Red" Garrett, who played 23 games for the NY Rangers during the 1942–43 season, was killed in action off the coast of Newfoundland on November 25, 1944. The American Hockey League's Rookie of the Year award is named in his honor.

Joseph Turner, a promising goaltender with Hall-of-Fame potential who played briefly with the Detroit Red Wings was killed in action in Holland on January 12, 1945, although his death was not officially recorded until December 19th of that year.

Another ice hockey star who paid the ultimate price defending his flag was Russ McConnell, who set the college hockey trail on fire as a member of the McGill hockey club from 1935 to 1939. In one of his last games wearing the McGill uniform, McConnell established a record for most points in a game when he recorded seven goals and three assists while playing against Harvard. McConnell enjoyed the experience so much, he went out and equaled the feat, this time collecting a balance beam-perfect five goals and five assists against the University of Montreal.

McConnell never reached the pinnacle of the NHL, however. His promising hockey career came to a tragic conclusion when he was killed in action. On September 7, 1942, his ship was torpedoed in the Gulf of St. Lawrence.

First hockey player to be awarded Canada's Medal of Bravery
The Humble Hero

1999

ABOVE: Much like Willie Trognitz, Joe Turner never hesitated to serve his fellow man. An outstanding goaltending prospect, Turner helped guide the Indianapolis Capitols to the Calder Cup championship in 1942. He joined the US Army shortly after the conclusion of the season and was killed in action some time in January of 1945.

Willie Trognitz was a burly no-nonsense battler who was best known as a one-man on-ice wrecking crew during his career. While toiling for Dayton of the International Hockey League in October of 1977, he was suspended for life by the IHL for seriously injuring Port Huron's Archie Henderson in a post-game altercation. He continued to play in the short-lived Pacific Hockey league, but when that fledgling loop folded in 1979, Trognitz returned to his hometown of Thunder Bay, Ontario, and joined the Canadian Coast Guard.

Like many "enforcers" who cause nothing but havoc on the ice, he was a soft-spoken guy off the pond who was always willing to lend a helping hand. Those hands came in, well, handy on October 30, 1996. On that evening an American tourist boat that went by the handle *Grampa Woo* was ripped from its mooring during a severe storm. Trognitz and his crew aboard the cutter *Westfort* joined another Coast Guard cutter, the *Glenda*, in a brave attempt to save the crew of the distressed ship. Battling gale-force winds of over 60 mph and 10-foot waves, the two-man crew were saved, although they had to abandon their ship and make a dramatic and dangerous leap from the sea-soaked deck of the *Woo* to the heaving deck of the *Glenda*.

Trognitz and the other five members of the Coast Guard crew were awarded Canada's Medal of Bravery in 1999.

First NHL trainer to serve in Vietnam

How I Spent My Summer Vacation

1968

BELOW: Clint Malarchuk owes his life to the quick thinking and calm demeanor of Buffalo trainer and Vietnam vet Jim Pizzutelli.

J im Pizzutelli, who is remembered best for playing a pivotal role in saving the life of Buffalo Sabres goaltender Clint Malarchuk, spent his summer vacation after graduation in 1968 doing a tour of duty in Vietnam.

Perhaps it was the experiences he faced in Vietnam that allowed him to be so cool under fire when he raced onto the ice to tend to the injured Buffalo netminder and discovered that Malarchuk was only seconds away from bleeding to death.

During a game against St. Louis on March 22, 1989, Blues' forward Steve Tuttle collided with Sabres defenseman Uwe Krupp and was sent flying into the Buffalo crease and goaltender Clint Malarchuk. As he was being upended, Tuttle's skate blade severed Malarchuk's jugular vein. Some quick and calm work by trainer Pizzutelli stemmed the flow of blood until the doctors could whisk the stricken netminder off the ice and rush him to hospital. Malarchuk spent only one night in hospital and was back in uniform guarding the Buffalo crease two weeks later.

Shakers, Breakers and Money Makers

First player to score 50 goals in a season
The Sweetest Herb

1938–39

ABOVE: The Great One, Wayne Gretzky, owns or shares 47 different NHL records, including the all-time mark for goals, assists and points in both the regular season and the playoffs.
ABOVE RIGHT: Herb Foster won three consecutive EHL scoring titles during his career with the Atlantic City Sea Gulls.

When Maurice "Rocket" Richard scored 50 goals in 50 games for the Montreal Canadiens during the 1944-45 season, most experts were convinced that the Rocket had established a record that would never be broken. As we all know, it's been obliterated numerous times, but the fact that he managed a goal-a-game pace is still an impressive achievement. However, Richard wasn't the first player to reach the 50-goal plateau in a single season, nor was he the first to average a goal-per-game.

That honor is bestowed on Herb Foster, an offensive wizard who tallied at least 20 goals in 10 different seasons, totals he would surely have added to had his career not been interrupted by the start of World War II. Although he suited up for only five NHL games during his career, Foster was the "Wayne Gretzky" of the old Eastern Hockey League while toiling with the Atlantic City Sea Gulls. Foster led the loop in goals in four consecutive campaigns from 1936 to 1939 before moving up the professional ladder to join the NY Rangers system. In 1938-39, Foster became the first player to score 50 goals in a single season, when he lit the red lamp 52 times in 52 games.

First rookie to score on each of his first four shots

Trigger Happy

1996

BELOW: Jan Caloun's accuracy mark still hits the bull's eye in the NHL record books.

On March 18, 1996, a young rookie from the Czech Republic named Jan Caloun made his NHL debut with the San Jose Sharks in a game against the Boston Bruins. Caloun made an impressive initial impact, slapping home his first NHL goal on his only shot on goal during the game. In his second game, against the Winnipeg Jets, Caloun fired two shots towards the Jets' net and, remarkably, both shots found the back of the net, giving the rookie three goals on his first three shots. Caloun then completed his march into the NHL record books as the most accurate rookie sniper in NHL history by scoring his fourth goal on his fourth NHL shot in his next game against Calgary. He completed the season with eight goals on only 20 shots on goal, giving him an accuracy rating of 40 percent.

First pro player to win three consecutive Stanley Cup titles

A Loan, Never Lonely

1922

ABOVE: Was it luck or was it fate? Eddie Gerard already had a pair of Stanley Cup wins on his resume when fate gave him a third championship. So, try to explain the hand that lady luck dealt to Doug McKay (Detroit–1950), Chris Hayes (Boston–1972) and Steve Brule (New Jersey–1990). They each played only one game in the NHL and still got their names etched on the Stanley Cup.

I t isn't very often that a player whose team has already been ousted from the playoffs gets the opportunity to win a Stanley Cup championship in the same year. But that's what happened to Eddie Gerard.

After helping the Ottawa Senators win a pair of back-to-back Stanley Cup titles in 1920 and 1921, Gerard found himself on the sidelines in 1922 after the Senators were dislodged from their Stanley Cup perch by the Toronto St. Pats.

Toronto went on to face the PCHA's Vancouver Millionaires in the 1922 Stanley Cup challenge series. In game three of the best-of-five set, Harry Cameron, one of the St. Pats top performers, was injured. The Toronto brass, sensing they had nothing to lose, asked Vancouver manager Lester Patrick if they could use Eddie Gerard as Cameron's replacement. Incredibly, Patrick gave the St. Pats permission to dress the Ottawa superstar.

In game four, Gerard played in perfect harmony with his new teammates and was a key factor in helping the St. Pats demolish their Western opponents by whitewashing the West-coasters 6-0. Apparently, that goose egg soured Mr. Patrick's love of "the amateur code" and he advised the St. Pats that Mr. Gerard would not be allowed to perform his magic for the Toronto team in game five. By now, however, the tides had turned and the St. Pats easily broke the Millionaires' bank with a 5-1 win. Since Gerard had played in a game during the Stanley Cup finals, he was credited with being a member of the Stanley Cup champion Toronto St. Pats. With that credential on his resume, Gerard became the first professional player to win three consecutive Stanley Cup titles.

First player to be an All-Star in five different leagues

They Call Me Mr. Gump

1950, 1951
1954, 1964, 1968

BELOW: Gump Worsley as a member of the NY Rovers.
BELOW RIGHT: Wendell Young displays his version of a "full house." Young is the only player to win a major championship in four different leagues.

They don't make 'em like Lorne "Gump" Worsley anymore. A roly-poly fellow with a sharp wit and a trigger temper, Worsley was the last Hall-of-Fame goaltender to play without a mask. When questioned about his lack of facial protection, Worsley snapped, "Anyone who wears [a mask] is chicken. My face is my mask."

The Gumper was one of the finest "custodians of the corded cottage" ever to stand between the pipes, and he has the scars and the used train tickets to prove it. The Gumper spent more time traveling the highway between the NHL and the minor leagues than a trucker with a deadline. And he was the star of the show in almost every arena he played in. The proof is in the history books. Worsley is the only goaltender to be honored as a First Team All-Star in five different professional leagues: Eastern Hockey League (1950); United States Hockey League (1951); Western Hockey League (1954); American Hockey League (1964) and National Hockey League (1968).

For good measure, Gump also made the Pacific Coast Hockey League's 2nd All-Star in 1952.

First player to play for All "Original Six" teams

In Lynn We Trust

1953

BELOW: Craig Berube
has played for five different
NHL clubs during his
17-year NHL career.

BELOW RIGHT: Vic Lynn
wheels away from a Black
Hawks defender during
his final full season with
the Toronto Maple Leafs
in 1947-48.

For decades, hockey historians have pilfered through documents and newspapers trying to find those players who were, at one time or another, the property of all six (Boston, Chicago, Detroit, New York, Montreal, Toronto) teams that were members of the league in what is always referred to as the Golden Era.

Until recently, researchers were content that they had uncovered three players — Bronco Horvath, Dave Creighton and Vic Lynn — who belonged to that exclusive club. However, in 1999, an even more fascinating discovery was made.

After carefully scrutinizing newspapers from the 1942–43 season, sleuths found reports that a rookie in the NY Rangers system named "Lynn" was called up to the big club as an injury replacement. Most historians assumed this couldn't be Vic Lynn, since his name did not appear in any of the NHL's official game sheets from that season. Yet, almost all the newspaper accounts of the game make a mention of the young busher who didn't look out of place among the "big guys." Finally, esteemed hockey analyst and historian Brian McFarlane contacted Mr. Lynn, who confirmed he did play one game with the NY Rangers.

So how could such an obvious statistic be overlooked? Because of the complications caused by World War II, it was inevitable that some official game sheets were misplaced, or perhaps were never filed. When Lynn was traded to Chicago on January 3, 1953, and suited up the following night for a game against Detroit, he completed his journey through every NHL port. So for the record, Mr. Lynn played with the NY Rangers (1942-43), Detroit Red Wings (1943-44), Montreal Canadiens (1945-46), Toronto Maple Leafs (1946-1950), Boston Bruins (1950-1952) and the Chicago Black Hawks (1953-1954).

First Rookie of the Year to be traded in the same season

Here I Am, Gone!

1954

t was the battle between the "haves" and the "have-nots" that led to Ed Litzenberger being traded midway through his Calder Trophy-winning rookie season in the NHL. In the mid-1950s, the Chicago Black Hawks were a pitiful on-ice sight, not that many people bothered to attend their games. Attendance was so sparse that the club even played some "home" games on the road in an effort to put some cash into the coffers. When the NHL brass met to discuss the situation, it was agreed that the more prosperous NHL teams (in terms of talent, not finances) would help out the "weaker" links, specifically the collapsing club from Chicago. The Montreal Canadiens stepped up to the plate and in 1954 dished over a promising young winger named Ed Litzenberger. The Habs could afford to deal a potential rookie-of-the-year candidate away because they had names like Rousseau, Marshall, Goyette and Talbot waiting in the wings. So, Litzenberger was expendable and he became the only player in the history of the NHL to win the Calder Trophy after being traded during his rookie season.

First player to be dubbed "The Babe Ruth of Hockey"

The Dye Is Cast

1921

ABOVE: Super-sniper Babe Dye, who captured a pair of NHL scoring titles in 1923 and 1925, became the first player to score nine goals in the Stanley Cup finals during the Toronto St. Pats championship run in 1922.

ABOVE RIGHT: Dye, who signed with Chicago after the Leafs released him, suffered a broken leg in training camp in 1927. The injury virtually ended his athletic career.

Usually Howie Morenz gets the nod for being the first hockey player to be dubbed "The Babe Ruth of Hockey." And make no mistake, Morenz filled arenas from Beantown to Broadway with his dazzling displays of speed and skill. But, he wasn't the first skater to be compared to the Sultan of Swat.

In the early 1920s, before Morenz started blazing his own trail, Cecil "Babe" Dye was the NHL's reigning sharpshooter. But Dye earned his nickname "Babe" because of his clout wearing cleats, not his skills donning skates. Dye, who also played football in the league that eventually become the CFL, was a three-sport star who was one of the most popular players with the Buffalo Bisons of the International League.

In 1921, Connie Mack was ready to pay $30,000 to the Bisons for Dye's rights, but the Buffalo club needed the Babe to put fans in the seats and cash in the coffers. It turned out to be a wise move, because Dye continued to excel in his summertime job. In 1923, Dye batted .318 and clouted 16 round-trippers, but he never did get the opportunity to play in the majors. He continued to dabble in minor-league baseball throughout much of his NHL career and retired with a career batting average of .311 proving he was one of hockey's finest "diamonds in the rough."

First player selected in NHL draft to play pro hockey and baseball
Wing and a Prayer

1981

BELOW: Kirk McCaskill poses for the lens during his one season with the Winnipeg Jets farm club in Sherbrooke, Quebec. He is the only Major League Baseball player to be drafted by a NHL team and play a full season of professional hockey.

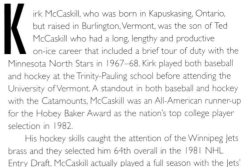

Kirk McCaskill, who was born in Kapuskasing, Ontario, but raised in Burlington, Vermont, was the son of Ted McCaskill who had a long, lengthy and productive on-ice career that included a brief tour of duty with the Minnesota North Stars in 1967–68. Kirk played both baseball and hockey at the Trinity-Pauling school before attending the University of Vermont. A standout in both baseball and hockey with the Catamounts, McCaskill was an All-American runner-up for the Hobey Baker Award as the nation's top college player selection in 1982.

His hockey skills caught the attention of the Winnipeg Jets brass and they selected him 64th overall in the 1981 NHL Entry Draft. McCaskill actually played a full season with the Jets' AHL affiliate in Sherbrooke during the 1983–84 season, recording 10 goals and 22 points. Following that brief on-ice sojourn, McCaskill adopted baseball as his #1 sport and went on to win 106 games in the majors, the second best total of all-time for a pitcher born in Canada.

McCaskill, who recorded 17 wins for Anaheim in 1986 and a 15-win campaign in 1989, placed his name in the Major League record books when he allowed back-to-back home runs by Ken Griffey Jr., and Ken Griffey Sr. It was the first and only time in baseball history that a father-son combination hit home runs in the same game.

Two of today's top Major League Baseball stars have a hockey connection that involves Canada and the crease. Colorado's Larry Walker, a seven-time Gold Glove winner and the National League MVP in 1997, was a goaltender on the same Ridge Meadows club as future Boston Bruins star Cam Neely.

Cory Koskie, who anchors the hot corner for the American League champion Minnesota Twins was also a goalie until he traded his catching glove for a baseball glove. Koskie spent two seasons guarding the crease for the Selkirk Steelers of the Manitoba Junior league before turning his attention from the rink to the diamond.

First player selected in NHL draft to win the Cy Young Award

This Lefty Was Right

1984

I n his senior year at Billerica High School in 1984, Tom Glavine was selected as the Boston Globe's Division I high school player of the year after leading his conference in scoring with 44 goals and 41 assists. He was also a four-time All-Conference All-Star in baseball.

In 1984, Glavine was selected by the Atlanta Braves in the 2nd round of the Major League Baseball Draft and chosen in the 2nd round of the NHL Entry Draft by the Winnipeg Jets. Although he truly loved both sports, Glavine decided on baseball as his sport of choice. "I just felt, being a left-handed pitcher, I had a little better chance of making it to major leagues in baseball," Glavine recalled in 1992.

Glavine proved to the sporting world that his intuition was wise. He went on to record five 20-win campaigns, and to win a pair of Cy Young Awards as then top hurler in the National League in 1991 and 1998.

Although he was never drafted by the NHL, Orel Hershiser could handle a puck as well as he could throw a slider. Hershiser, who won the Cy Young Award and was named the World Series MVP in 1988, was a graduate of the Philadelphia Little Flyers organization, one of most respected and productive minor league programs in the United States.

Freewheeling Firsts
Fictitious Facts

BELOW LEFT: Billy Burch, the Yonkers Yankee.
BELOW RIGHT: Ken Doraty scored the winning goal in the second longest overtime game in NHL history.
OPPOSITE LEFT: Fred Hucul was selected to the WHL's All-Time All-Star Team.
OPPOSITE RIGHT: Alex Smart was the scout who discovered future 500-goal scorer Luc Robitaille.

First U.S.-born player inducted into Hockey Hall of Fame

Billy Burch was born in Yonkers, New York, and played his entire career with the Hamilton Tigers, who later relocated to the Big Apple and were named the NY Americans.

First player to be an NHL All-Star as both a forward and defenseman

Dit Clapper was a Second Team All-Star as a forward in 1931 and 1935, before turning his attention to the defensive side of the ledger. He was equally successful on the blueline, earning First Team All-Star accolades in 1939 and 1940 as well as a Second Team berth in 1944.

First player to take a penalty shot

Armand Mondou took the first penalty shot in NHL history but Ralph "Scotty" Bowman was the first player to score, plugging the pill past Alex Connell on November 13, 1934.

First rookie to score three goals in his first NHL game

Discounting those players who played in other professional leagues before entering the NHL, Alex Smart of the Montreal Canadiens was the first player to record a hat-trick in his first NHL game on January 14, 1943, in a 5-1 victory over Chicago.

First player to score a goal in his only NHL game

On December 13, 1930, Roly Huard of the Toronto Maple Leafs scored the opening goal in a 7-3 loss to the Boston Bruins. He was the first player in NHL history to score a goal in his only NHL appearance. Six decades later, Detroit defender Dean Morton scored a goal in his one and only game with the Red Wings during the 1989–90 season.

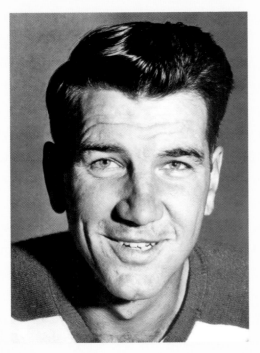

First player to score an empty-net goal in the NHL

Chicago's Clint "Snuffy" Smith scored into an empty Boston net at 19:12 of the 3rd period to give Chicago a 6-4 win vs. Boston on November 11, 1943.

First player to score three overtime goals in one game

From 1928–29 until 1942–43, NHL teams played a full ten-minute overtime period if the game was tied after 60 minutes. On January 16, 1934, Toronto Maple Leaf forward Kenny Doraty became the first — and only — NHL player to register a hat-trick in overtime when he scored three goals in extra time against the Ottawa Senators in a 7-4 Leafs win. The tallies came at 00:45, 1:35 and 6:45 of overtime.

First NHLer to play Major League Baseball

James Riley played NHL hockey with both the Chicago Black Hawks and Detroit Cougars during the 1926–27 season and played Major League Baseball with the St. Louis Browns (1921) and the Washington Senators (1923).

First player to return to major junior after a full season in the NHL

Sylvain Cote spent the 1982–83 season with the Hartford Whalers before returning to junior with the Quebec Remparts in 1983-84.

First player to go 15 years between goals in the NHL

Fred Hucul scored 5 goals for Chicago in 1952–53 but didn't score another NHL goal until 1967–68, when he was a member of the St. Louis Blues.

First goaltender to go 18 years between NHL appearances

Moe Roberts, who had brief sojourns with Boston and the NY Americans until 1933–34, was employed as the Chicago Black Hawks' assistant trainer and practice goaltender when he replaced the injured Harry Lumley in goal on November 25, 1951.

First rookie to score an NHL goal before scoring a goal in junior hockey

Kris Draper was signed as a free agent by Winnipeg and began the 1990–91 season with the Jets before being sent to the Ottawa Senators on the OHL.

First player to collect 200 points in a season

Joe Hardy, who played 63 NHL games with the California/Oakland Seals, made hockey history when he collected 208 points with the North American Hockey League's Beauce Jaros in 1975–76.

CHAPTER 3

THE GAME

his is the section where we look at the mechanics of the sport from the inside. The evolution of equipment has played an essential role in the growth of the game, and you'll discover some interesting new twists and turns as you uncover the people responsible for adding new dimensions to the sport. From cow pies to pucks to Plexiglas, all of the essential firsts are related here.

We'll open up the rule book, look inside the press box, peer into the television camera and gaze into the future. The bench bosses, prized players, press and people who have played instrumental roles in guiding the game from pastime to prime time all take a well-deserved bow in this section.

And while the sport has never gathered much respect in Hollywood, the game has always been on the silver screen and a surprisingly large number of former and current skaters have taken a star turn or two in Tinseltown.

OPPOSITE: As "rookies" in the WHA's inaugural season, Guy Smith (#19) and Ted Green were exposed to see-through boards, blue pucks, bad ice, big brawls and bouncing checks.

BELOW: The NHL erected nylon mesh screens behind the goal area prior to the 2002-03 season to protect fans from flying pucks.

As we look inside the game, we see innovative coaches who changed the way the game was played, inspirational motivators who turned nerves on the inside into numbers on the scoreboard.

No sport can maintain success unless it reaches its audience promptly and accurately, so we honor the scribes who scripted the game, the commentators who called the games and the engineering geniuses who brought us the game on radio and television.

And then there are the men in stripes. The referees never get an even break in the arena, but we pay them homage here. Legendary whistle blowers like Fred Waghorne and Bill Chadwick were both instrumental in improving the game because they realized their role as on-ice arbitrators was more than whistle tooting. It was also improvisation, adjustment and adaptation.

Here is the game. It's all yours.

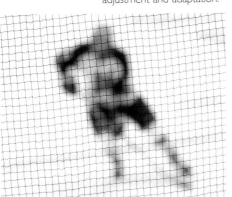

Coaches

First coach to lose a game before he coached a game

Skinning Fats

ABOVE: Venerable veteran Johnny Bower, seen here receiving some in-crease advice from coach Billy Reay (left) early in the 1958-59 season, stood in for Punch Imlach and served as bench boss for the Leafs during the third period of a game against the NY Rangers on April 2, 1966. **ABOVE RIGHT:** Alex Delvecchio compiled a 82-131-32 wins-loss-tie record in his 245-game career as the Wings' bench boss.

When the Detroit Red Wings decided to place head coach Ted Garvin in the "where are they now" file after only 11 games behind the Motown bench, the club brass asked 24-year veteran Alex "Fats" Delvecchio to take over the coaching reins. Delvecchio, who was still active as a player, agreed to take on the formidable task and journeyed down to the Olympia on November 7, 1973, to assume his new duties. But there was a problem. The Red Wings had neglected to file Delvecchio's retirement papers in time for him to coach the game. So, when "Fats" arrived at the rink, he was informed he was temporarily grounded as the new pilot of the Red Wings.

The situation should have placed owner Bruce Norris and g.m. Ned Harkness in an embarrassing predicament. Instead, they asked the very man they had dismissed only hours earlier to stay around for one more game. The freshly deposed coach wasn't keen on the idea, but since he was still being paid by the club, he agreed to honor the plea. There was one caveat in Garvin's favor. Since Delvecchio was now "officially" the coach, the result of the game — win, lose, or draw — would be attached to Delvecchio's coaching resume. And considering the sorry state of the team, that result was almost guaranteed to be a loss.

Well, the Wings didn't disappoint the prognosticators. They went out and played their usual tired and uninspired game. With three minutes remaining in the game and the Wings trailing Philadelphia 4-1, Garvin fled the scene. Injured Wings forward Tim Eccelstone took over until the final whistle. When Delvecchio finally took his spot behind the pine three nights later, he already had a perfect loss-win-tie record.

First coach to pull his goalie for an "extra attacker"

Yank Me, Please

1941

BELOW: Paul Thompson assumed coaching duties of the Chicago Black Hawks midway through the 1938-39 campaign. In his first full season behind the bench, Thompson led the team to a 23-19-6 record, totals that earned him a third berth on the NHL All-Star team, and his first and only nod as a coach.

The first coach to be credited with pulling the goaltender and replacing him with an extra attacker in an attempt to tie the game was former Chicago Black Hawks coach Paul Thompson. In the dying moments of the Hawks' last game of the season on March 16, 1941, Thompson yanked goalie Sam LoPresti and sent out a forward in a vain attempt to rally the troops into scoring the tying tally.

Old Sam probably didn't mind getting the opportunity for a brief rest. Only 12 days earlier, Sweet Sam established an NHL record that, if there's any justice, will never be broken. On March 4, 1941, in a game against the Boston Bruins, LoPresti stopped 80 of the 83 shots the Beantowners drilled at him and in a 3-2 loss. Boston's Johnny Crawford was asked afterwards if he thought LoPresti was good or lucky. Crawford replied, "He was good alright. If he hadn't have been good, he would've been dead."

LoPresti may have learned a lesson or two about survival by escaping that parade of pucks. In February of 1943, while serving in the US Merchant Marines, LoPresti's ship was torpedoed by the enemy and he survived 42 harrowing days and nights in a lifeboat until he was rescued by an Allied patrol boat.

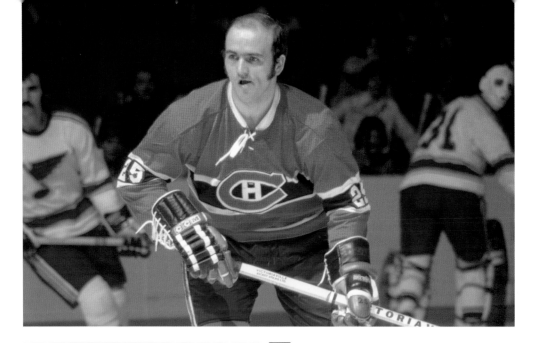

First coach to change lines "on the fly"

Keeping the Horses Fresh

1923

ABOVE: Jacques Lemaire was one of the smartest, most calculating and intelligent players to ever wear the bleu, blanc et rouge of the Montreal Canadiens. Much like the innovative Lester Patrick, Lemaire has the rare ability to translate the skills he possessed as a player into tangible and teachable theories that he can convey to his players as a Stanley Cup-winning coach.

RIGHT: George Owen was a college All-American in hockey, baseball and football. Hockey became his professional sport of choice when Boston owner Charles Adams (Harvard/Class of 1888), offered him a $25,000 signing bonus to join the Bruins in 1928.

eorge Owen

The first coach to be credited with changing lines and defensemen while the play was still in progress was Odie Cleghorn, the pilot of the Pittsburgh Pirates, the first American-based team to compete in the NHL. Cleghorn knew his veteran squad wasn't as talented as the other NHL clubs, so he came up with an idea to even up the playing field. Instead of using the same six or seven players in every game, Cleghorn decided to form forward lines and use them in tandem. By constantly changing his forward units, he kept some aging legs young and allowed grizzled warriors to be highly competitive.

The honor for becoming the first bench boss to establish set forward lines and alternate them throughout the game, though not when the puck was still in play, is usually bestowed on Lester Patrick. The Silver Fox came up with his ploy when he was guiding the Victoria Maroons. Up against the unenviable task of facing the swift and offensively potent Montreal Canadiens in the 1925 Stanley Cup finals, Patrick knew his squad could only compete with the Hustling Habs if he had fresh horses. So, while the Habs stayed with their tried-and-true policy of playing the Joliet-Morenz tandem all night long, Patrick rolled his lines like clockwork. As a result, Victoria became the last non-NHL team to drink champagne from the Stanley Cup.

Both of those men get the accolades, but as Paul Harvey would say, here's the rest of the story. One man did both before the other two.

The first coach to implement the idea of changing lines during play was William H. Claflin, the bench boss of the Harvard University hockey team. On March 3, 1923, in a game against Yale University, Claflin decided to unleash his new strategy. The Crimson changed the game of hockey forever by substituting entire forward lines instead of individual players. As the Yale team watched in bewilderment, Harvard defeated their rivals as team captain and multi-sport superstar George Owen scored in overtime to give the Crimson a 2-1 victory.

The first coach to refuse
to take a penalty shot

Needy, But Never Greedy

2003

Most lovers of the world's fastest game are in agreement that the penalty shot is the most exciting and exhilarating play in the game. It is a pity, because penalty shots are very seldom called by the on-ice arbitrators. So when a coach actually refuses the opportunity to take a penalty shot that has been granted to him, it's a real eye-opener. But, on January 6, 2003, that's exactly what Jack Parker of the Boston University Terriers did. And he showed a little class in the process. With less than five minutes remaining in the third period of the Eagles' game against Northeastern, Boston University was awarded a penalty shot when freshman Brad Zancanaro was upended by goalie Keni Gibson. At the time, the Eagles were winning by a 7-2 margin, so Coach Parker refused to accept the penalty shot.

Now, most of the scribes in attendance were surprised at Parker's decision, but most were even more shocked when Coach Parker told the assembled media after the match that he was perfectly within the rights of the rule book to deny the need to take a penalty shot. To illustrate his point, Parker produced a copy of the NCAA guidelines and pointed out Section 6, Subsection (A). It states that in a situation where an infraction of the rules calls for a penalty shot not involving a major penalty, the non-offending team shall be given the option of accepting the penalty shot or having a minor penalty assessed.

After more than 50 years in the game, old Jackie proved he still knew the rules, but more important, still appreciated the true meaning of sporting spirit and fair play.

First person to coach one team and play for another – in the same league!

Double Duty

1938

BELOW: Before Len Burrage (here with Harringay) became a hockey hero in Britain, he was a member of the Moncton Hawks club that won back-to-back Allan Cup titles in 1933 and 1934.

Len Burrage may not be a familiar name but he occupies a special place on the throne of hockey history. The former resident of Winnipeg, Manitoba, cemented his place in hockey folklore by becoming the first man to play for one club and coach another — in the same league!

At the beginning of the 1937-38 season, Burrage was already employed as a defenseman for the Harringay Racers, one of eleven teams in the British National League. When the Manchester Rapids — another BNL team — found themselves in desperate need of a new coach early in the season, they asked for and received permission to hire Burrage, as long as Len continued to honor his commitment to the Harringay club.

So, Burrage took on the task of balancing his duties as a defenseman for one club and juggling lines for another. There was one more complication both he and the league had to come to grips with, and that was the scheduled match between Harringay and Manchester slated for March 2, 1938.

Numerous suggestions were entertained. One of the more unique takes had Burrage playing a period for each team and coaching in the third stanza or simply flipping a coin to decide which team would have his services. It was even proposed that he remain neutral and referee the game.

In the end, the BNL stepped in and ruled that since Burrage had started the season as a member of the Harringay club, he should play the game with the Racers. So he did.

At the conclusion of the campaign, Burrage returned to North America and ended his career as a member of the EHL's Washington Eagles.

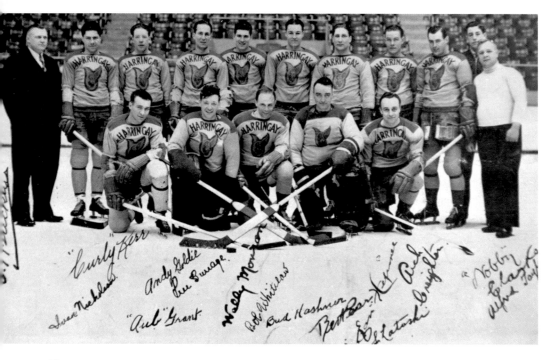

ABOVE: In 2002–03, Bob Hartley became the first Stanley Cup-winning coach to pilot two different NHL clubs in the same season.

RIGHT: Glen Sather (second from left) and goaltender Jacques Plante (left) both played, coached and managed in the WHA.

First coach to sign himself to a professional contract

Don't Put Me In, Coach

1979

OPPOSITE: 2000 — Larry Robinson threw the sinking New Jersey Devils a Stanley Cup lifeline.
BELOW: 1993 —Jacques Demers raises the Silver Chalice above his head.
RIGHT: 2003 — Darryl Sutter became one of three men to coach two different NHL clubs in the same season.

When the Quebec Nordiques arrived at the Quebec Coliseum on March 18, 1979, to play the Edmonton Oilers, Coach Jacques Demers found himself in one pickle of a predicament. Due to injuries and illness, the Nords didn't have the minimum 15 players needed to play a WHA game. That left Demers with only one possible solution. Since he was also serving as the team's general manager, Demers signed himself to a five-game tryout contract, donned a uniform and coached the match in full gear. He never hit the ice, though, because he wasn't needed. Despite having only enough healthy bodies to reach a quorum, the Nordiques drained the Oilers 7-2.

The Media

As Our Radio Friends See Us

The Maple Leaf Management respectfully requests that you patronize our advertisers

The first hockey
broadcast on radio
Who Knew It, It Wasn't Hewitt

1918

ABOVE: As this
artwork aptly illustrates,
Hewitt also recited
wrestling rhetoric and
provided pugilistic prognos-
tications for avid boxing
enthusiasts.
ABOVE RIGHT: Foster
Hewitt stationed at the
microphone in his famous
gondola high above the
ice surface in Maple Leaf
Gardens.

What's likely the most famous phrase in the hockey
lexicon? "He shoots, He scores!" Those four famous
words were first uttered by the most esteemed
hockey broadcaster of all time, Hall-of-Fame member Foster Hewitt. However, Mr. Hewitt is also given the nod
as the first person to broadcast a live ice hockey match on the
radio. But this is one instance where the sands of time have
eroded the facts.

The first radio broadcast of a hockey match occurred on
February 18, 1918. Norm Albert was the man behind the micro-
phone and the game action he described was a contest between
North Toronto and Midland. North Toronto won the game by a
convincing16-4 score, with future Hall-of-Fame member Lionel
Conacher providing the dramatics by potting four goals.

For the record, Hewitt's first broadcast was aired on
March 22, 1923. With only a few hours' notice to prepare,
Hewitt did the play-by-play account of an intermediate play-off
game between Kitchener and Toronto Parkdale at the old
Mutual Street arena in Toronto. Using an ordinary telephone as
a microphone, Hewitt spent three hours on the air describing
the on-ice action through three periods of regulation time and
almost three periods of overtime.

First television broadcast
Shadows on Ice

1938

Most hockey scholars point to a game between the NY Rangers and the Montreal Canadiens that was played on February 25, 1940, as the first hockey match to be seen on television. An experimental station known as W2XBS, which is currently known as WNBC-TV in New York City, was responsible for providing the live feed for the game. The Rangers downed the Habs by a count of 6-2 in a game that was watched by approximately 300 people.

However, the world's first live transmission of an ice hockey match on TV actually took place in England on October 29, 1938. The second and third periods of the Harringay Racers 7-3 victory over Streatham in the British National Tournament was shown live from the Harringay Arena in London. The feed was transmitted to the BBC studios at Alexandra Palace and sent out over the airwaves.

The initial Canadian Broadcasting Corporation (CBC) NHL hockey broadcast was aired on October 11, 1952, and it featured a match from the Montreal Forum, where the Habs were entertaining the Detroit Red Wings.

HOCKEY BROADCAST
HOT STOVE LEAGUE
— ON THE AIR —

The NHL's First Mascot
Who is that Masked Man?

1984

Who was the first person to create a cartoon character, craft a colorful costume and make a memorable debut as a mascot in a NHL arena? Well, that depends on what you read, where you read it and who you believe. One thing is certain — the first mascot to entertain NHL audiences was a mangy mutt named "Harvey the Hound," who made his first appearance in the old Calgary Corral, the home of the Calgary Flames, in 1984.

From that point on, the facts get fuzzy. Some sources claim a fellow named Glenn Street created Harvey and played him with panache for seven years. Other historians insist that it was Grant Kelba who originated the canine character and portrayed him for 15 years from 1984 to 1998.

Now, this debate would have no point or interest if Harvey hadn't found himself pasted on the front page of the sports section in every major newspaper on January 22, 2003. In a game against Edmonton the previous evening, Harvey positioned himself behind the Oilers' bench and proceeded to toss a tirade of taunts and issue an itinerary of insults at the Edmonton team. Ultimately, Oilers' coach Craig MacTavish, tired of the Harvey's hounding, grabbed the mascot, ripped the tongue out of his mouth and tossed it into the crowd.

Harvey was reprimanded by the club, scolded by the league and reminded that mascots are mute characters that are better seen and definitely better not heard.

Oh, by the way, both Kelba and Street share credit for creating and playing the role of Harvey the Hound. However, since the duo went their separate ways, the trail of truth has been tainted. The identity of the person inside the suit these days remains a mystery.

First hockey movie starring John Wayne

Pass the Puck, Pilgrim

1937

ABOVE: John Wayne wasn't the only Academy Award-winning actor to be cast against type and star in a Hollywood hockey movie. Oscar® winners Paul Newman (*Slapshot*), Russell Crowe (*Mystery, Alaska*), Karl Malden (*Miracle on Ice*) and Meryl Streep (*The Deadliest Season*) were all fixtures in films that featured flashing blades and flying fists.

In 1937, John Wayne played one of his more challenging roles, not due to the depth or difficulty of the script or story, but because he had to perform this demanding role while balanced precariously on skates. And the Duke didn't skate. The movie was entitled *Idol of the Crowds* and Wayne starred as a retired hockey player named Johnny Hanson. It's interesting to note that Nancy Dowd, who wrote the script for the movie *Slapshot*, borrowed the Hanson name for the motley trio of brothers who wreak havoc throughout the flick.

Although Hollywood has never exactly embraced hockey as a box office bonanza, there have been a few cashbox surprises that featured hockey. In the multi-kleenex weeper *Love Story*, Ryan O'Neil's character, Oliver Barrett, plays a mean game of shinny as a smooth skating star of the Harvard University Crimson. It has grossed a handy sum of 106 million dollars since its release on December 16, 1970.

And then, of course, there was *The Mighty Ducks*, a Disney feature that deposited $50 million more in the Disney bank account. *The Ducks* wasn't the Disney Studios' first spin around the ice hockey arena. That honor belongs to *Hockey Homicide*, an eight minute animated cartoon that was released on September 21, 1945. Featuring a star turn by Goofie, it depicts the story of that big on-ice showdown between the Pelicans and the Aardvarks. It's actually a brilliant commentary on the sport, as cynical as *Slapshot* and almost as funny.

The first hockey movie

Ice and the Silver Screen

1899

BELOW: Like Thomas Edison, Rene Lecavalier was a groundbreaking pioneer who crossed cultural boundaries and set new broadcasting standards. His description of Henderson's winning goal in the 1972 Canada-Russia Summit Series —"Et le but de Henderson!" still elicits chills among the hockey faithful in Quebec.

The Internet Movie Database lists a 1930 feature entitled *The Battered Mug* as the first film released to theaters that involved the sport of ice hockey. In reality, it was not a movie, it was a film of Foster Hewitt doing the play-by-play of a game between the Toronto Maple Leafs and the Montreal Maroons that was being broadcast over the radio. The teams are competing for the Stanley Cup, which according to the press release of the day, was "that ancient trophy which is affectionately known all over Canada as 'The Battered Mug.'"

The film was lost in the dusty vaults of time before being resurrected by film director Donald Britten, who included it in his groundbreaking documentary *Dreamland: A History of Early Canadian Movies 1895-1939*.

The first known footage of ice hockey action was actually filmed in 1899 by Thomas Edison himself. The clip, a brief ten-second piece of celluloid shot by one stationary camera, featured a group of railroad workers playing a spirited game of shinny on an outdoor pond.

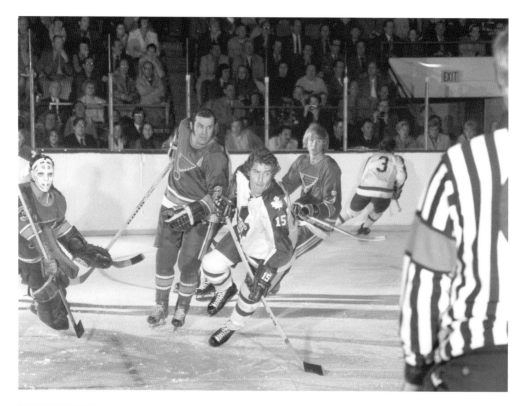

First made-for TV
ice hockey movie
Mike and Meryl

1977

ABOVE: Brian "Spinner"
Spencer (#15) wheels away
from a pair of St. Louis
Blues defenders (Noel
Picard #2 and Garry Unger
#7) in search of a loose
puck. Spencer was a loose
puck himself—a talented
but tormented individual
who longed for tranquillity
but only found tragedy.

The first "made for TV" movie by a USA network to focus on ice hockey was a 1977 release entitled *The Deadliest Season*. Starring Michael Moriarty, the film is renowned because it is the first on-screen performance by Meryl Streep.

Moriarty plays a hard-hitting but clean-playing defenseman named Gerry Miller. However, after repeated requests and threats from team management to toughen up play with aggression and anger, he succumbs to the pressure and becomes the on-ice goon he never wanted to become. That new style wins him adoration from the fans and a few extra bucks from the owners, until Miller kills another player in an on-ice altercation and is arrested and tried for manslaughter.

The first "made for TV" movie about a player who made his NHL debut on the same night his father was killed by police was *Gross Misconduct*, the tragic story of former Toronto Maple Leafs and Buffalo Sabres scrapper Brian "Spinner" Spencer.

On December 12, 1970, the night his son was making his NHL debut with the Toronto Maple Leafs, Roy Spencer — armed and dangerously angry because the local TV network was not showing the Leafs game that evening — was shot by police after he threatened employees at a Prince George, BC, television station. In the game his father failed to see, Spencer scored a pair of goals and was named the 1st Star of the game.

Brian Spencer's life and career were permanently scarred by that event, all of which is detailed in the movie. He was eventually shot and killed himself in a roadside robbery in Florida on October 3, 1988.

First hockey movie directed by an Academy Award winner

The Roughhouse Hockey Players who Curse a Lot and Play Dirty — Japanese translation for the title of the movie *Slapshot*

1977

BELOW: Jack, Steve and Jeff Hanson roar up the ice looking for trouble and expecting to find it. The heroes of *Slapshot* are also known as Three Stooges on Ice, The Trio of Terror, Weird, Weirder and Weirdest, The Dim Some Threesome, The Ice Men Dumbeth, The Three Fools Without Rules and The Brain Dead Brothers.

After directing *Butch Cassidy and the Sundance Kid* and *The Sting*, two films that were critically acclaimed and accumulated huge box office returns, Academy Award-winning director George Roy Hill became the talk of Tinseltown when he announced that his next two projects were films about a stunt plane pilot named Waldo Pepper and a slapstick comedy about ice hockey entitled *Slapshot*.

It was the hockey film that gathered most of the attention, since not only was it centered on a mostly obscure sport and was scripted by a first-time screenwriter, it was also written by a woman named Nancy Dowd. Women didn't play hockey. What could they possibly know about the game?

It was a stroke of genius on Hill's part to realize that it was the very fact that Dowd saw hockey from an entirely different perspective that made the whole project so appealing. Dowd knew the game, and she enlisted her brother Ned to do the "leg" work and the hard research.

Ned Dowd was a pretty fair puck handler at Bowdoin College, and he spent three years toiling in the deepest dungeons of the darkest minor leagues to complete his research on the rich and varied assortment of characters who are quite content to ride the buses on the lowest rung of the professional ladder just for the love of the game. Most of the characters in the movie are based on real players Dowd met and played with during his three year tutorial in the minors.

Michael Ontkean, who was an offensive dynamo with the University of New Hampshire in the late 1960s before turning his talents to another kind of stage, starred in the timeless classic that still has them roaring in the aisles to this day.

Silver-screen shorts
Spotlight Shenanigans

BELOW TOP: Blake Ball was recruited to play a small — but important — role in the movie *Slapshot,* appearing as Gilmore Tuttle, "the all-time penalty minutes leader for the Federal League."
BOTTOM: Howie Young was a bucking bronco on the ice and a wild stallion outside the rink. Still, he was also a dependable defenseman, marketable movie star and rodeo rider.

First hockey player to appear in a soap opera
Ron Greschner of the NY Rangers appeared on the soap opera *Ryan's Hope* in July of 1980.

First hockey player to appear in a movie with Frank Sinatra
Howie Young, who was billed as John Howard Young, appeared in the war flick *None But the Brave* with Sinatra, Clint Walker and Tommy Sands. Rafer Johnson, a former NFL linebacker, also had a role in the movie.

First movie to feature ten pro hockey players with speaking roles
Slapshot — Dave Hanson (NHL, WHA), Steve Carlson (WHA, NHL), Jeff Carlson (WHA), Blake Ball (WHA, AHL), Connie Madigan (NHL), Joe Nolan (EHL), Mark Bousquet (NAHL), Don Dufek (NCAA, drafted by Detroit, played NHL football with Seattle), Ned Dowd (NAHL) and Ross Smith (WHA/NAHL)

First NHL player to marry a *Playboy* Playmate of the Year
Charlie Simmer was married to Terri Welles, *Playboy* magazine's Playmate of the Year for 1981.

First hockey player to host *Saturday Night Live*
Wayne Gretzky hosted the irreverent weekly satire show on May 13, 1989, with musical guests Fine Young Cannibals.

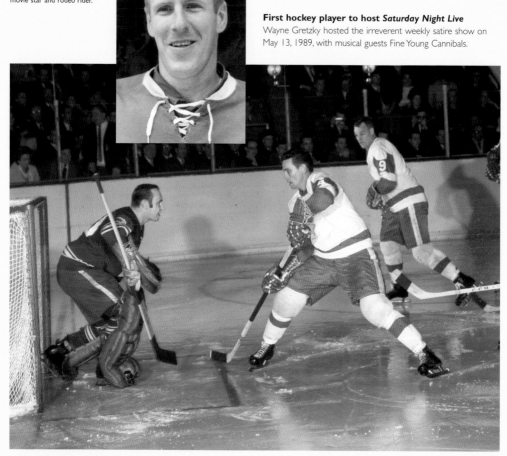

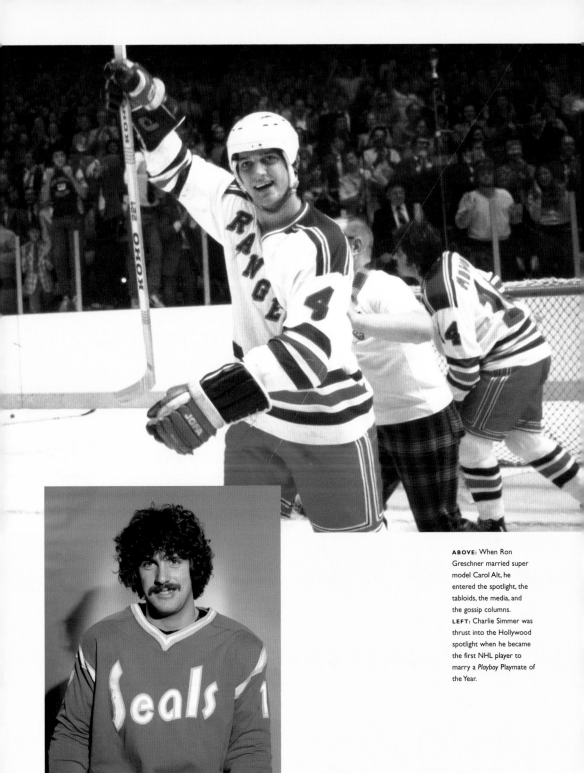

ABOVE: When Ron Greschner married super model Carol Alt, he entered the spotlight, the tabloids, the media, and the gossip columns.
LEFT: Charlie Simmer was thrust into the Hollywood spotlight when he became the first NHL player to marry a *Playboy* Playmate of the Year.

Men in Stripes

First referee to drop the puck
Saving Shins to Save Face

1900

BELOW: Fred Waghorne, hockey's first and finest on-ice arbitrator, believed a referee should be well-rounded in the rules and well groomed in his appearance.

Fred Waghorne was one of hockey's first and finest referees. A cool customer with a keen eye, he was also responsible for introducing numerous innovations to the game. He was the first on-ice judge to use a bell instead of a whistle, he was the first to pull out the rule book to determine proper rulings and he is often credited for being the first referee to drop the puck to commence play.

Prior to 1900, the referee would place the puck on the ice between the opposing players selected to "take the draw," yell "Play" and jump out of the way. Even the most agile of on-ice whistle tooters had trouble escaping the slashing, slicing and stabbing as the combatants flailed about attempting to secure possession of the puck.

During a game in 1900, Waghorne lost his temper and grabbed the two gentlemen who were about to commence their stick-swinging battle for the puck. He positioned them a foot or two apart and commissioned them to place their sticks on the ice and not to move a muscle until the puck he was about to drop between them touched the ice surface. By the time rubber reached rink, Waghorne and his shins were safely out of the way. He had saved face by creating the "face off."

There's little doubt of the validity of Waghorne's story, but some historical pundits claim that it was a Winnipeg on-ice arbitrator who invented the face off. Since his name goes unrecorded and the match where he administrated his solution to one of the game's more frustrating problems is also unknown, it's Waghorne's bugle that hits the right notes to this off-ice observer.

If the origin of the face off is in question, the first game to feature NHL players using the "original" face off is not. During the 1993–94 NHL lockout, various NHL players organized teams and played three-on-three games to raise money for charity and stay in shape. In those matches, the puck was simply tossed into the corner after a stop in play and play continued, not unlike the rules still used wherever road hockey is still played.

Mr. Waghorne, the popular official referee for the O. H. A. is a veteran Hockey and Lacrosse player. His experience makes him an expert on skates and the fact that he has used none but "STARR" skates for years is strong testimony to their high qualities.

F. C. WAGHORNE.
OFFICIAL REFEREE FOR THE O. H. A.
He has used "STARR" skates exclusively for years.

First referee to use hand signals

The Fickle Five Fingers of Fate

1912

t was only after he hung up his whistle for good that referee Bill Chadwick informed the sporting public why he always chuckled when a player called him blind. That's because, in a sense, he was.

A promising amateur player, Chadwick's career was cut short when he sustained a serious eye injury when he was struck flush in the eye by a stray puck during practice. Hours later he learned he had permanently lost all vision in the afflicted eye.

The injury that brought an early conclusion to his career as a player was the stepping stone that helped lead him to the NHL. After replacing a sick referee during an EHL game, Chadwick quickly rose through the ranks. In 1940, at the age of 24, Chadwick was promoted to the NHL, working as a linesman in his initial campaign before becoming a referee the following year.

It was shortly after becoming the chief whistle tooter that Chadwick introduced his most famous innovation. Using baseball umpires as his resource, Chadwick decided to implement a series of hand gestures to illustrate the calls he was making on the ice. Chadwick would clutch his wrist to signal a holding penalty, fan his arms out like a baseball umpire to signal a no goal call, strike his leg with a karate-like motion to signal tripping or strike his arm in the same manner to signal slashing.

The initial reaction to Chadwick's gestures was that many media members labeled him a "show-off." However, the fans reacted favorably to Chadwick's method of signaling penalties.

In those days, the public-address systems were barely audible, but every fan who could see Chadwick's hand motions knew immediately what call was being made on the ice.

No matter how inventive Chadwick was, he cannot claim to have been the first referee to use hand signals. H.H. (Henry) Roxborough, one of the sports pioneering historians wrote, "In 1912 referees began using signals to inform spectators of the nature of offences. For a minor, the ref raised his left hand; for a major, his right hand; for a match foul, he raised both hands." Bill was best, but he wasn't first.

First referee to use the rule book in a game
Have Logic, Will Travel

1900

ABOVE: Paul Stewart, a rambunctious and rowdy troublemaker during his playing days in the WHA and NHL, has proven himself to be Fred Waghorne's equal in terms of poise, preparation and precision.

I n the infancy of the sport, referees were constantly being challenged for their in-game decisions, both by the roaring denizens in the seats and the stick-wielding combatants on the ice. If a team didn't feel that the on-ice judge was up to snuff, he could be, and sometimes was, replaced.

As you have read, one of hockey's foremost on-ice arbitrators in the early years of the game was Fred Waghorne, who was not only innovative, but also had a keen sense of logic. And he used it to defuse a potentially riotous situation.

When Waghorne was overseeing a senior hockey match in Belleville, Ontario, in 1900, one of the Belleville forwards unleashed a shot that plunked off the goalpost. At this time, pucks were manufactured by gluing two separate rubber pieces together. On this particular evening when the disc caught the iron, it split into two pieces. One half caromed into the corner while the other half bounced into the net.

Both teams immediately surrounded Waghorne, awaiting the arbitrator's decision. Was it a goal or wasn't it?

The crafty referee raised a single finger to his lips, called for "order in his courtroom" and pulled a fresh copy of the first hockey rulebook (published only months earlier) from his waistcoat. He opened the volume to the proper page and pointed out a paragraph that stated: "The puck must be one inch thick and three inches in diameter."

Since the object that had entered the goal was not one inch thick, it was not a legal puck. To the dismay of the crowd but to the satisfaction of the players, on-ice justice had been served. No goal had been scored.

First active players to serve as linesmen in an NHL game

Have Stripes, Will Serve

BELOW TOP: Mickey Vulcan — sans stripes.
BOTTOM: Gary Howatt doing what he did best — causing havoc in the crease and trouble in the trenches.

They probably shouldn't even have attempted to play a hockey game on the night of January 15, 1983. Although a classic winter blizzard had shut down much of the eastern seaboard, both the Hartford Whalers and the New Jersey Devils were able to reach the Hartford arena, so the game was set to begin — until it was discovered that both referee Ron Fournier and linesman Dan Marouelli could not be found.

Ron Foyt, the one linesman who did make it to the rink, hatched a clever plan. Consulting the rulebook, Foyt discovered that he was allowed to act as referee and could appoint a player from each club to serve as linesmen. Since both Fournier and Marouelli were "on route," the league allowed the plan to proceed.

Gary Howatt of the NY Islanders and Mickey Vulcan of the Whalers were both nursing minor injuries that didn't hamper their ability to skate or see, so they were recruited as voluntary linesmen. Both were only too happy to assist Foyt because they realized it was an opportunity for both "offensively challenged" players to enter the NHL history books.

The first period went by without any controversy, although both Howatt and Vulcan admitted they were "sweating in their stripes." Luckily, the two tardy officials arrived during the first intermission and replaced the nervous volunteers. Howatt and Vulcan remain the only two modern-day players ever to serve as officials during a regular season NHL game.

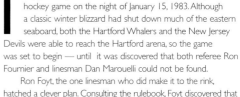

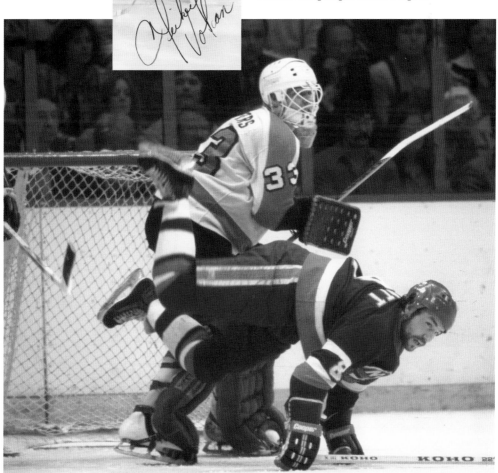

First amateur officials to work an NHL playoff game
Donut Gate

1988

BELOW TOP: Edmonton's Pat Conacher goes noggin-to-noggin with referee Don Koharski in a vain attempt to reverse an on-ice decision by the striped arbitrator. **BOTTOM:** Jim Schoenfeld, seen here during his tempestuous tenure behind the New Jersey Devils bench, became the first NHL player to record a version of Bob Dylan's "All Along the Watchtower" and actually have the guts to release it in 1973.

"You're crazy! I didn't push you! Get another donut, you fat pig." — Jim Schoenfeld. That comment triggered one of the most embarrassing events in NHL history. On May 6, 1988, the New Jersey Devils were soundly licked 6-1 by the Boston Bruins in game three of the Wales Conference finals. Jim Schoenfeld, the Devils' bench boss, felt referee Don Koharski made a number of questionable calls against his club and confronted him after the final whistle.

The two men went toe-to-toe and chest-to-chest and somehow Koharski lost his balance and toppled to the floor. When Koharski claimed he was pushed, Schoenfeld uttered the quote inscribed above, plus a few expletives best left to the imagination of the readers.

Although the area was crowded with media and officials, everyone had a different opinion of exactly what had happened. As far as the league was concerned, physical contact had occurred and the Jersey bench boss would have to be suspended for at least one game pending a review.

New Jersey g.m. Lou Lamoriello may have been a NHL rookie at his post, but he was a savvy veteran when it came to playing bureaucratic angles. First he filed a lawsuit against the NHL's ruling and then found a judge who agreed to issue a restraining order that negated the NHL edict and allowed Schoenfeld to continue coaching until the legal system determined his status.

When the New Jersey coach showed up at his post prior to game four, the officiating crew slated to work that night refused to step on the ice until he was removed from the arena. Despite hours of debate between the league brass, the officials' union and the Devils, no compromise could be reached. Adding to the drama was the fact that NHL president John Ziegler was on a "secret sabbatical" and could not be reached. This forced the NHL officials on hand to do some quick fence-mending.

Desperate to get the game underway, the NHL had no alternative but to hire three 50-year-old amateur officials to work the game. Referee Paul McInnis had to borrow a pair of blades from New Jersey forward Aaron Broten but at least he got to wear the stripes. Linesmen Vin Godleski and Jim Sullivan were forced to wear yellow jerseys and green sweatpants until regulation uniforms could be obtained. The fact that the Devils went on to record a 3-1 victory is a forgotten aspect of what became known as the "Yellow Sunday" fiasco that went into the record books as a victory for the Devils, a loss for the Bruins and a massive headache for the NHL.

And to this day, no one has yet disclosed the whereabouts of NHL president John Ziegler on that bizarre spring Sunday evening.

First referee to penalize Superman
Is There a Phone Booth Handy?

1979

ABOVE: Ted Garvin, who compiled back-to-back 40-goal seasons as a member of the IHL's Sarnia Sailors, experienced his greatest off-ice success as the coach of the IHL's Toledo Goaldiggers.

One of the oddest coaches ever to patrol the pine was Ted Garvin, a former NHL coach with Detroit and a wild man behind the bench who was known to litter the ice with debris of every description. In 1979, while coaching Toledo in the IHL, Terrible Ted became upset with one of referee Sam Sisco's decisions. After waving his arms frantically like some prehistoric bird and uttering odd yelping noises, Garvin climbed onto the boards and began to disrobe. When he was down to his undershirt, which was emblazoned with a large Superman crest, Sisco thumbed the coach for unsportsmanlike conduct and gave the Clark Kent wanna-be two minutes in the sin-bin.

Coaches rarely get penalized in a game, but when they do, the results are often disastrous. Michael Therrien, former bench boss of the Montreal Canadiens can attest to that. Late in game four of Montreal's Eastern Division semi-final series against Carolina in 2002, Therrien was given a bench minor penalty by referee Kerry Fraser after making an obscene gesture after Fraser had called a penalty on the Habs. Carolina, down 2-1 in the series and 3-0 in the game, scored a pair of goals on the ensuing power play and later won the match in overtime. The Canadiens went on to lose the series in six games. Therrien was vilified by the Montreal media and most scribes believe it was his playoff blunder that led to his being fired during the 2002–03 season.

Referee roulette
Whistle While You Work

BELOW: John Ashley was once a promising defenseman in the Toronto Maple Leafs farm system.
BELOW RIGHT: Former player and novice referee King Clancy studies the rulebook.

First referee to work the seventh game of a playoff three times in one year
John Ashley worked the seventh and deciding game of the 1971 quarterfinals, semi-finals, and finals. Then he retired.

First drafted NHL player to become a linesman
Drafted 115th overall in 1971 by the NY Rangers, Wayne Forsey became a linesman after retiring as a player and officiated in the NHL from 1979 to 1988.

First drafted NHL player to become a referee
Drafted 148th overall by Detroit in 1986, Dean Morton has two claims to fame. He is the only defenseman in NHL history to score a goal in his one and only NHL game, and he is the first player drafted by a NHL team to become a NHL referee.

First modern-era NHL players to become referees
In addition to Morton, Paul Stewart (21 NHL games, 65 WHA games) and Kevin Maguire (260 NHL games) — who were both signed as free agents — are the only other modern-era players with NHL experience to become NHL referees.

First Hall of Fame referee to come out of retirement
During a NY Islanders/Atlanta Flames tilt on December 30, 1978, Hall of Fame member Frank Udvari came out of the stands and out of retirement to replace injured referee Dave Newell. Borrowing a pair of blades from Islanders' star Bryan Trottier, Udvari officiated for the rest of the game, calling two penalties and disallowing one goal — by Trottier, naturally.

First NHL referee to fire a goal judge
During a game between the Colorado Rockies and the St. Louis Blues on April Fool's Day in 1979, referee Greg Madill effectively fired goal judge Rod Lippman. After Lippman turned on the red light to signal a goal for two shots that didn't even hit the net and later failed to "light the lamp" for a pair of legitimate goals, Madill had him removed from his post.

ABOVE: Gordie Howe
(#9) drives Toronto's
Gord Hannigan in the
boards as referee Frank
Udvari climbs the screen
to escape being flattened
by the rambunctious Red
Wings forward. Udvari
was one of the first referees
to use this method of rising
above the action to avoid
on-ice collisions.

RIGHT: Rough and tough
Kevin Maguire muscled
his way up the pro hockey
ladder before turning in his
socks for stripes.

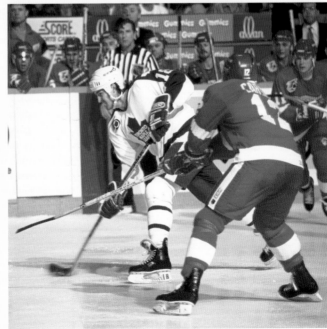

Rules and Equipment

First "official" game played with rules
Somebody Had to Do It

1875

It was a trio of inventive students at Montreal's McGill University who were responsible for organizing the first hockey game that was played with a viable set of rules. The riotous on-ice sporting activity that eventually would become known as ice hockey was first played by a select group of undergraduates at McGill in the mid-1870s. It is generally accepted that the basics for the game were introduced to these fine fellows by J.G.A. Creighton, who carted the game up the St. Lawrence from Halifax to Montreal.

Under his guidance, a game was arranged that used the rules he had learned in Nova Scotia. Scheduled for March 3, 1875, the game was advertised in the newspaper and the results were published the following day. Creighton captained the team that represented the Montreal Amateur Athletic Association, while Fred Torrence headed the crew representing the Victoria Skating Rink, where the match was played. Creighton's nine-man side defeated Torrence's lads by a count of 2-1.

Three of Creighton's students, W.L. Murray, W.F. Robertson and R.F. Smith, were responsible for drafting the first standardized set of rules by carefully scrutinizing the playing laws for English rugby and field hockey. With this information in their database, they jotted down a series of rules for ice hockey. The game has grown since then.

The First hockey puck
Putting Cows Out of Work

1886

BELOW: This ancient hunk of vulcanized rubber was the puck used in the Stanley Cup playoff game between the Montreal Shamrocks and Winnipeg Victorias on January 29, 1900. In a tense tussle, the Winnipeg sextet eked out a 4-3 win over their eastern combatants.

When the game of hockey was in its infancy, the common game piece used was a frozen cow pie, which seemed to come custom-made from the local dairy farms. When the game moved inside, a vulcanized Indian rubber ball was utilized. The players at this time were true amateurs, and most of them were university students, but they found themselves scratching for rent money because the uncontrollable bouncing ball they used to play this new sport they loved broke so many windows in the rink where they played.

For a period, a wooden puck was used, and for the most part it worked quite well, although the pace tended to be slow and ponderous. Then a genius whose name escaped the historians' ledgers cut the top and bottom halves of one of those wildly bouncing balls and the first "real" hockey puck was born.

The Goodyear Company, which invented vulcanized rubber in 1839, caught wind of this rapidly evolving sport and in the early 1880s began producing the first factory-made hockey pucks. The first recorded use of a hockey puck was in Kingston, Ontario, when teams from the Royal Military College and Queen's University first met in 1886. In the same year, the Amateur Hockey Association of Canada adopted the vulcanized disc as the official puck of the association.

First time a hockey puck was used in a game
Disc? Oh!

1875

The first documented proof of a flat disc being used in a game of ice hockey can be found in the published reports about the infamous game played on March 3, 1875. The *Montreal Gazette* reported that "A game of hockey will be played at the Victoria Skating Rink this evening between two nines from among the members. Good fun can be expected, as some of the players are reputed to be exceedingly expert at the game."

The first puck to become a TV star was a charming creature named Peter Puck, who was created by cartoon wizards at the Hanna-Barbera studios. In 1974, the NBC network used Mr. Puck to explain the rules, nuances and history of the game to the American audience who were mostly unfamiliar with the game.

Scotty Connal, the executive producer of NBC Sports explained the Peter Puck phenomenon this way, "When we asked Hanna-Barbera to create a little cartoon character on ice who would explain hockey in a humorous, entertaining manner, we never dreamed he'd become the most popular segment of our intermissions."

Well, Peter may have been popular, but the puck wasn't. NBC cancelled its coverage of NHL hockey after one season. Peter Puck lived on in Canada on CBC TV and in print through the words of Brian McFarlane, noted hockey historian and broadcaster.

First use of goalie pads

When An Old Cricketer Leaves His Crease

1896

BELOW TOP: George "Whitey" Merritt, who is credited with introducing leg pads to the goaltenders' arsenal, may have actually borrowed his innovation from an Aboriginal team that barnstormed around Manitoba in the late 1890s.
BOTTOM: Rejean Lemelin deflects the puck just beyond the reach of Edmonton's Wayne Gretzky during game three of the 1998 Stanley Cup finals. Lemelin's revolutionary Aeroflex pads may have increased his mobility, but they couldn't derail the Edmonton victory train, as the Oilers convincingly flattened the Bruins to capture their 4th championship in five years.

On Valentine's Day eve in 1896, hundreds of die-hard, feisty and fervent ice hockey fans gathered in Montreal to witness the one-game, winner-take-all Stanley Cup Challenge match between the defending champion Montreal Vics and a sordid squad of upstarts from the wilderness of Winnipeg.

When George "Whitey" Merritt, the goaltender of the Winnipeg side, skated to his position between the posts, a hush fell over the crowd. Merritt was wearing protective pads on his legs! Outside his trousers! In fact, Merritt was wearing white cricket pads on his legs.

While Merritt played a steady, strong game and certainly had a psychological advantage over his adversaries, it was the skating and defensive skills of his teammates that allowed Winnipeg to defeat the defending champs 2-0 and cart Lord Stanley's silverware back to the prairies.

But was Merritt the first goaltender to wear pads? Bill Fitsell, an acclaimed sports journalist and first president of the Society of International Research (SIHR) notes that there are several photographs from the early 1890s showing goaltenders wearing outside leg protection. But since Merritt caused such a stir on the front, sports, business and fashion pages, and helped his club capture the most revered trophy in hockey, he grabs the nod here.

The first modern goalie pads were designed and created in 1924 by Emil "Pop" Kenesky, who modified cricket pads by stuffing and widening them to approximately 12 inches. They caught on and were used by a majority of goaltenders until Boston netminder Rejean Lemelin showed up one evening modeling a set of synthetic pads called "Aeroflex." They weighed less than 1/3 of his old pads, were more flexible, didn't retain water and allowed him to move with much more dexterity. They are now the "pad" of choice for every young and old goaltender and have helped improve and extend the careers of numerous twine-tenders.

First use of a goalie mask

The Proboscis That Changed Hockey History

BELOW TOP: This crude and rather rude leather contraption was the bulky facial protection that Clint Benedict wore in the final days of his NHL career. **BOTTOM:** Curtis "Cujo" Joseph models the modern-era goalie mask — a form-fitting fiberglass helmet that protects the head, a stainless steel cage that protects the face while providing an excellent line of vision and a polyethylene attachment that connects to the helmet and hangs below the mask to provide neck protection.

Jacques Plante, arguably the greatest goaltender in the history of the sport, is commonly given credit for being the first goaltender to wear facial protection in a NHL hockey game. It is true that after Mr. Plante took a brisk backhander off the blade of Andy Bathgate flush in the face on November 1, 1959, he donned a facemask for the rest of that match and, except for one game later in that season, for the rest of his career. It was one of the pivotal moments in the history of the game, but it was not the first time that a netminder wore facial protection.

Most hockey historians point to Clint Benedict as being the first crease cop to wear a mask. Certainly, he was the trendsetter as far as the NHL is concerned. On January 7, 1930, Montreal Canadien superstar Howie Morenz plunked a puck off Benedict's nose and cheekbone. This marked the umpteenth time that Benedict's proboscis had been broken during a game, so he fashioned a crude yellow-leather contraption to protect his swollen nose. Depending on which published report you trust, Benedict's innovation was based on either a football face guard or the facial protection worn by sparring boxers. Regardless, after wearing the gadget for five games, "Praying Benny" took another blow to the blower and quit playing altogether.

Since the facemask is somewhat of a fashion statement, it shouldn't come as a surprise to learn that the first goalie to wear a mask was actually a lady. In 1927, Elizabeth Graham, who patrolled the crease for the Queen's University women's team, donned a fencing mask during her stay between the pipes for the Golden Gaels and wore it for the remainder of that season.

First appearance of the modern hockey net
The Stocking Exchange

1899

ABOVE: Before goal judges were given their own off-ice cubicles, they stood directly behind the net. Standing in such close proximity to the goal wasn't as dangerous as one may assume. In the early years of the game, players rarely raised the puck. The only thing this fur coat-clad official had to fear was frostbite and shin burn.

Three or four separate branches claim they helped design the frame of the modern hockey net. One story has a clever goalie named William Fairbrother from Beamsville, Ontario, suggesting that fish netting be draped over the goal posts in 1897. Newspaper accounts suggest the new nets were favorably received. There's also a claim from historians that fishermen in Paris, Ontario, originated the idea in 1896 after seeing too many disputed goals disrupt a playoff series between Paris and Hamilton.

Hockey folklorists from the East Coast area contend that resourceful hockey-loving fishermen from Nova Scotia created the prototype of the modern hockey goal. A report in the Halifax newspapers on January 6, 1899, mentions that the use of the Nova Scotia Box Net during a game between two Halifax clubs allowed the goal judge to stand behind the net, which had never been done before.

In 1899, Quebec goalie Frank Stocking brought his designs for a new hockey net to the executive of the CHL. On December 26, 1899, the Montreal Shamrocks and the Montreal Victorias tried out the new cages, liked them and the design was accepted and used during the 1899–90 season.

But it is the "modern" innovator we're after here and that is Hall-of-Fame member Percy LeSueur, who added a crossbar to the frame in 1912, giving the net the same basic shape and design still used today.

First use of a curved stick
Banana Blade Buddies

1960

BELOW: Both Andy Bathgate (top) and Stan Mikita (bottom) make convincing arguments to support their claim to fame as the inventor of the bent blade.

As the NHL considers passing legislation to increase the amount of curve allowed on a hockey blade, the debate over who originated the curved stick has heated up. Two men claim responsibility for the innovation, former NY Ranger superstar Andy Bathgate and Chicago Black Hawks center Stan Mikita.

Bathgate's bend on the story has him experimenting with curved blades as a youngster in the 1940s. "I had a curved blade playing road hockey when I was a kid," Bathgate recalls, "and I thought, with this big hook I can raise the puck." Bathgate's method was simple — he heated the blade in a bucket of hot water until it was soft enough to bend.

Stan's story is that he invented the blade by accident. "It was toward the end of practice and I was bushed," Mikita recalled. "My stick cracked, so out of anger, I slapped the puck against the boards, hoping to break the stick all the way. Well, it didn't break, but I noticed the puck took off a little different. Later, I ran a couple of them under hot water, bent them and taped 'em up. Then I went out on my own and just started shooting the puck, wondering what might happen. The puck seemed to jump off my stick quicker and with more force and it gave my slap shot a knuckleball effect."

Regardless, the era of the banana blade was born. Soon, every player in the league was bent out of shape. With pucks flying crazily in all directions and the graceful art of the backhand shot all but eliminated from the game, the NHL was forced to cut the craze. Prior to the start of the 1970–71 season, the league introduced new legislation that limited the curve on a blade to no more than a half inch.

But who was the first player to use a curved blade? Hall-of-Fame player, coach and manager Jack Adams always contended that Cy Denenny was the first player to use a curved blade in 1960, using the exact same method as described by Andy Bathgate. Adams went on to say that he tried the innovation himself, but he couldn't control his puck, his passes or his shots, so he dropped the idea.

First use of a helmet
Cover Me

1913

W hen you're dealing with a sport where the very origin of the game is still a topic of debate, it shouldn't be surprising that there are numerous other gray areas in the game's historical timeline. One of these has always been the first use of a helmet in an ice hockey game. Until now, that is.

The first recorded use of head protection can be found in accounts of the Pacific Coast Hockey Association during the 1913–14 campaign. In early December of 1913, Moose Johnson, who was toiling for the New Westminster Royals at the time, collided with teammate Art Throop and suffered a broken jaw. Never one to let a little fracture interfere with his livelihood, Johnson fashioned a crude-looking piece of headgear with a protective bar of some kind designed to relieve his aching lower jaw. When he skated onto the ice toting this contraption on his noggin, a lady fan who obviously felt that the modeling of fashionable headwear should be confined solely to women, reached over and tried to yank the offending bonnet from Johnson's head. Johnson's sole comment on the episode was that her attempts "hurt more than any hockey jostling."

Prior to the start of the 1979–80 season, the NHL passed a new rule that required all players entering the league after June 1, 1979, to wear proper head protection. Craig McTavish, who retired following the 1996–97 season, was the last NHL player to skate in a regular season or playoff game without wearing a helmet.

First puck to last through an entire NHL game

No Souvenirs

1979

BELOW: The actual origin of the word "puck" has never been firmly established, although most historians believe the term is borrowed from the Irish sport of hurling. In the lexicon of that game, the term "puck" refers to the act of hitting or striking the ball with the stick.

On November 10, 1979, the Los Angeles Kings and Minnesota North Stars played an entire game using only one puck. Whether it was a freak kind of miracle or a pitiful performance by two lower-level teams has never been firmly established, but the puck never left the ice surface during the entire game. That rare chunk of vulcanized rubber is now on display at the Hockey Hall of Fame in Toronto.

In the modern NHL, there are dozens of pucks "on ice," ready and waiting to be put in play. However, in the formative years of the NHL, there would often be only a rare pair of pucks available for each game. In fact when the puck left the playing surface, the fans were asked to find the disc and return it to the referee so the game could continue. And the fans often complied. One would imagine that there would be a number of occasions when a surly fan would refuse to do his duty, bringing a halt to the proceedings. Yet, the first time that an NHL game was almost derailed because of a shortage of pucks, the fans were not the culprits.

On February 26, 1926, the Toronto St. Pats were trailing the Montreal Maroons by a 4-3 count when they appeared to score the tying marker. However referee Bob Hewitson ruled the puck had never entered the net and waved off the St. Pats goal. As one can imagine, this caused a great deal of consternation among the Toronto faithful. During the donnybrook that followed Hewitson's controversial call, Toronto forward Babe Dye deftly plucked the puck from the scrum and refused to return it to the on-ice arbitrator until he reversed his decision. When Hewitson informed Mr. Dye that he would forfeit the match to the Maroons, Babe handed over the prized pill. The Maroons held on for the 4-3 victory.

Stats, Traps, Flaps, and Raps

First player to wear a triple-digit number
Too Wide On the Side

1986

ABOVE: Hockey's most admired uniform number was once #9, which was worn by Howe, Hull and Maurice Richard. Wayne Gretzky wore #9 throughout his minor league career, but when he joined the Soo Greyhounds in 1977, it was already claimed. He tried out #14 and #19 before settling on #99, and the rest is history. **RIGHT:** Wilf Paiement was the last player not named Gretzky to wear #99.

Mel Hewitt is the only professional hockey player to wear a triple-digit number on his uniform. As a member of the IHL's Salt Lake City Golden Eagles during the 1986–87 season, Hewitt wore #111 on his back. This caused great problems in the league office because the column used on the game sheets to record a player's uniform number wasn't wide enough to accommodate three digits. Because of mathematics and logistics, Hewitt was forced to wear the more conventional #19 for the remainder of the campaign. The same fate befell goaltender Rodun Gunn. When he tried to wear .45 on his back, league officials quickly stepped in and stripped the jersey off Gunn's back.

Gunn was a real pistol on the ice and a rare firecracker outside the rink. Blessed with a better sense of humor than skill, he became the first goaltender to propose to his girlfriend while she was singing the national anthem. Well, actually, it was after she sang the anthem, but let's not let the facts get in the way of a good story.

When his lady finished singing "The Star-Spangled Banner" before a game on January 7, 1999, Gunn skated towards her, dropped to one knee — or one pad in this case — and presented his loved one with a diamond ring. He then proceeded to allow four goals on the first four shots he faced so he would get the hook and spend the rest of the evening singing the "Wedding Bell Blues."

First non-goaltender to wear #1 in the NHL

#1 in Your Program

1926

The Montreal Canadiens are the most storied franchise in the history of the NHL, partially because of the club's respect for tradition and history. The club has also retired more jersey numbers than any other team in league history, which restricts the digits left for the modern player to choose from. But that doesn't explain why the Canadiens are the only team to have had three non-goaltenders wear #1 on their jerseys. Herb Gardiner displayed the single digit on his back in the 1926–27 and 1927–28 seasons. Marty Burke proudly wore #1 during the 1928–29 campaign and Babe Seibert donned the lone digit from 1936 to 1939. Of course, the Habs were also the first club to have three players wear #99, which was made famous a few decades later by Wayne Gretzky. Leo Bourgeault, Joe Lamb and Des Roche modeled the double nines during the 1934–35 season.

First player to be named 1st, 2nd and 3rd star in the same game

The Rocket's Ride

1944

ABOVE: Maurice "Rocket" Richard (left) shares a laugh with coach Toe Blake and Jean Beliveau.

On March 23, 1944, Montreal's fiery superstar Maurice "Rocket" Richard became only the second player in NHL history to score five goals in a single post-season game as he singlehandedly destroyed the Toronto Maple Leafs in a 5-1 Habs win.

Although the Rocket's five-goal performance wasn't a NHL first, the post-game accolades that awaited him would place him in the history books forever. After such a record-setting performance, Richard was confident he was going to be chosen as the 1st star of the game, so he waited in the dressing room for the announcement of the 3rd and 2nd stars of the match. Much to the surprise of the Rocket, and the assembled throng at the Montreal Forum, Richard was named as the 3rd star of the game. The Montreal multitude went mad with a wild chorus of boos and derisive commentary. It was only when Richard was also named as the 2nd star of the game that the audience began to catch on. When Foster Hewitt announced that Richard was also the 1st star of the game, the Forum erupted with an elongated ovation to salute their hockey hero.

First player to record 2,000 career points
The Guile in Guyle

1962

BELOW: Although he enjoyed remarkable success on the minor league circuit, Fielder failed to collect a single point during his brief NHL appearances with Detroit, Chicago and Boston.
BELOW RIGHT: The Great One and the Greatest — #99 and #9.

While the accolades for all-time hockey greatness are usually heaped upon Gordie Howe and Wayne Gretzky, there's one player who often gets left out of the loop. That player is Guyle Fielder, one of the finest playmakers to ever don a pair of skates and feather a picture-perfect pass to a teammate. Fielder is often left out of the loop because he never registered a single point in the National Hockey League. But in 1962 he became the first professional hockey player to accumulate 2,000 career points.

Fielder had his opportunities to make his name known in the big leagues, but circumstances and bad luck combined to keep him out of the NHL spotlight. Whatever the reason, it was a stroke of good fortune for hockey fans in outport hockey harbors like Seattle, Portland and Salt Lake City. He was the pre-expansion era's Wayne Gretzky — shifty, clever and always thinking two plays ahead, concentrating not on where the puck was, but where the puck was going to go. Perhaps it was the gods of the Bus Leagues who conspired to keep him as a big fish in a small pond, because fans in those towns were lucky enough to watch Fielder perform his on-ice magic on a nightly basis.

Although he was unable to hit the scoresheet in the nine NHL games he appeared in with Detroit, Chicago and Boston, Fielder was an offensive dynamo in the minor leagues. In the 1,487 games he played in the PCHA, WHL and AHL, Fielder scored 438 goals and added 1,491 assists. Tack on the 25 goals and 83 assists he collected in post-season play and you have a remarkable career total of 2,037 points.

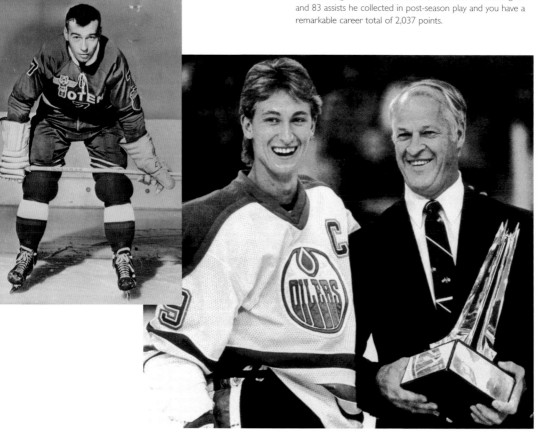

First hat trick with a hat
Haberdashery Happenstance

1946

ABOVE: Hockey's ceremonial tossing of the cap celebrates a three-goal performance by a hometown lad.

ABOVE RIGHT: When Alex Kaleta lit the lamp three times on January 26, 1946, the Black Hawks became the first NHL team club to have three different players register hat-tricks in three consecutive games.

It was all because Alex Kaleta wanted a new hat. When the trendy Black Hawks forward wandered into Sammy Taft's downtown Toronto haberdashery on January 26, 1946, he made an instant impression on Mr. Taft by using every bargaining tool at his disposal in a vain attempt to get a free chapeau. Since Sammy was a wee bit of a gambler, he promised the Black Hawks busher that if he managed to score three goals against the Leafs that night, he could have any hat in the house.

Now, Sammy was also an astute businessman and clever handicapper. Two Black Hawks marksmen had already notched hat tricks in the previous two games the team played, so the odds were in Sammy's favor. Kaleta scored his trio of goals, strolled into Sammy's store, selected the finest hat in the place and went on his merry way. It wasn't long before the print jockeys caught wind of the story and went to get Taft's take of the tale. When Sammy admitted, "Yeah, that was some trick he pulled to get that hat," the term "hat trick" was born.

First three-game career with three different teams

Stitch 'em and Stop 'em

1953
1956
1957

Until the NHL ruled that every team was required to have a second goaltender dressed and ready to replace an injured teammate prior to the 1965–66 season, every team dressed only one goalie. But it was the responsibility of the home team to have an alternate netminder in the stands ready and willing to don the pads and replace an injured cage custodian should he be needed.

Like most NHL clubs at the time, the tight-fisted Detroit Red Wings employed an assistant trainer who was adept at stopping pills and handing them out.

During the 1950s, that task was the responsibility of Ross "Lefty" Wilson, who served as the Wings' assistant trainer from 1950 to 1961. After enduring countless bumps, bruises, cuts, concussions, slashes and stitches, Wilson handed the duties to a youngster named Danny Olesevich and concentrated on being the Red Wings' main maintenance man from 1961 to 1982.

Although Wilson was a surgeon with a suture and a magician with the medicine, his greatest accomplishments came as an emergency goaltender pressed into service. He made his NHL debut on October 10, 1953, with 16 minutes of shutout goaltending in a 4-1 loss to Montreal. On January 22, 1956, Wilson stepped into the Toronto crease and stoned his Detroit "teammates" for the final eleven minutes of the contest. Wilson's career came to a close on December 29, 1957, with a 52-minute masterpiece as an injury replacement for Boston's Don Simmons. Although he allowed the first — and only — goal of his career, Wilson also earned his first decision in helping the Beantowners hold the Wings to a well-deserved 2-2 draw.

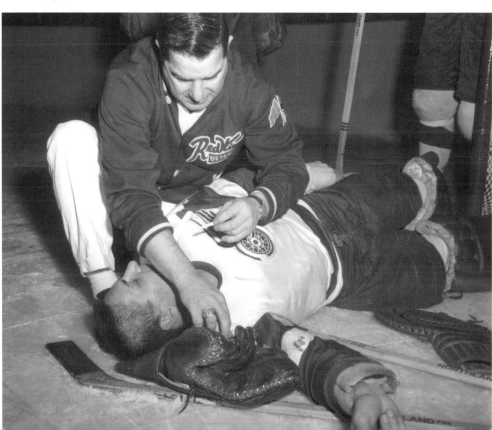

First use of the "neutral zone" trap
Kitty Bar the Door

1915

ABOVE: Always poised and prepared during his Hall of Fame career as a player, Jacques Lemaire continues to display the same dedication and attention to detail as a coach. In the 2003 playoffs, he helped the Minnesota Wild become the first team in NHL history to rebound from a three games to one deficit and win the series twice in the same playoff season.

Almost every shinny critic places the blame for the "trap" system of defense firmly on the shoulders of Jacques Lemaire, who used it to perfection in the New Jersey Devils' cruise to the Stanley Cup championship in 1994. But Lemaire can only share credit for the blame because he was just playing a modern game of "kitty bar the door."

The first evidence of a "trap" defensive system can be traced to one of the great architects of the sport, Art Ross. While he was traveling to Montreal with the Ottawa Senators for the 1915 NHA championship, Ross devised a new defensive system in his head.

Ross felt that the lightning-fast Montreal club could be neutralized only if there were three defenders positioned in close proximity to his team's net. One must remember, there was no forward passing in the game at this time. What Ross planned to do was cut off the parallel passing lanes and crowd the area in front of the net so the Habs couldn't use their speed.

The strategy worked to near perfection. Every time a Montreal attacker approached the net he was greeted by a horde of Senators defenders. The Ottawa club defeated Montreal by a tally of 4-1 in the two-game total-goal format. However, Ross' "trap" failed to work in the Cup finals when the Capital City lads traveled to British Columbia to face the Vancouver Millionaires. That series was played under Western rules, which meant that a seventh man — or a rover — was added to on-ice lineup. That enabled the Westerners to put the Puss 'n Boots to the Senators' "kitty" strategy and sweep the three-game series.

Famous firsts of futility
The Hall of Shame

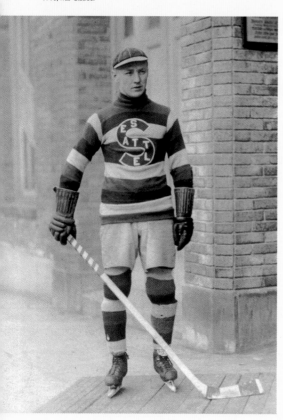

BELOW: In 1916, Cully Wilson became the first player to play on the West Coast one night and in Central Canada the next, which is impossible, of course. Yet, for years, Wilson has been credited with playing three games with Toronto during the 1915-16 season. However, ace researcher Joseph Nieforth discovered that the Wilson, who played for Seattle on January 25, 1916, was Cully and the Wilson, who played for Toronto on January 26, 1916, was Claude.

Many are called, few are chosen and some just don't get there. Just because a hockey player reaches the highest rung on the professional ladder and actually gets to play a game in the NHL, there's no guarantee that success will follow. Here are a few of the few who have reached the penthouse of hockey futility.

First player in NHL history to play 150 games without scoring a goal
On January 6, 2003, Carolina Hurricanes defenseman Steve Halko became the first player in NHL history to play 150 games without scoring a goal.

First player in NHL history to play 100 post-season games without scoring a goal
On April 17, 1996, Winnipeg Jets rearguard Craig Muni became the first player in NHL history to appear in 100 post-season games without scoring a goal.

First player to have a plus/minus rating of −80
Bill Mikkelson had the unfortunate task of manning the blueline for the 1974–75 Washington Capitals, the worst expansion team in NHL history. Mikkelson compiled a plus/minus rating of −82 during the season, but at least he had company. The four worst plus/minus ratings ever recorded were by members of the Washington squad that compiled a 67-5-8 loss-win-tie-record in their initial NHL season. Tom Williams (-69), Greg Joly (-68) and Mike Marson (-65) share in Mikkelson's pain.

First goalie to win 300 NHL games without winning the Stanley Cup
John Vanbiesbrouck won 374 games during his NHL career, but never found himself in the right place at the right time. If it's any consolation to the big "V," CuJo is closing in on his record.

First NHL player to collect 800 career points and never play in an All-Star Game
Some readers will argue that this isn't a mark of futility, it's a sign of good luck. Nevertheless, one of the finest European-trained players ever to skate in the NHL never had the opportunity to play in the game. Thomas Steen, who played his entire career in Winnipeg was a model of consistency and decorum during his 14-year stay in the prairie capital. Every other NHL player who collected at least 800 career points has participated in the NHL's showcase contest. So, in this case, the stamp of futility should go on the narrow-sighted selectors who overlooked Steen for so many years.

ABOVE: Steve Halko still doesn't know how, but he sure wishes he did.
ABOVE RIGHT: No one has been through what Bill Mikkelson has seen.
RIGHT: Craig Muni didn't think his post-season drought was funny.

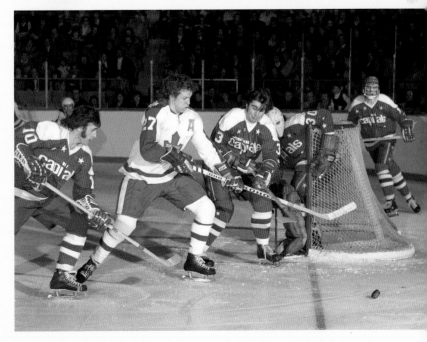

First hockey player to die as a result of an on-ice injury

Blood on the Ice

1905

BELOW: Although he wore a helmet throughout his college career, Bill Masterton (#19) played bare-headed when he joined the NHL's Minnesota North Stars in 1967. A graduate of the University of Denver, Masterton scored his first NHL goal and the first goal in the history of the Minnesota franchise on October 11, 1967, against St. Louis. He tallied 11 more goals before that fateful night in early January of 1968.

The first recorded incident of an on-ice fatality occurred on February 24, 1905, during a game between teams representing the towns of Maxville and Alexandria. There was a fierce rivalry between the two villages and when they met on the ice, fireworks of some kind were guaranteed. Part of the profile of their great distaste for each other was founded on religious and linguistic doctrines. Alexandria was populated by French Canadians who were mostly Roman Catholics. Maxville was largely an English Anglo-Saxon and Protestant town.

Moments after the opening draw, Maxville's Allan Loney decked Alcide Laurin with a swift jab to the jaw and a timely tap to the temple. Laurin hit the ice with a resounding thud and died five minutes later. Loney was indicted on a murder rap, but all charges were dropped and the case dismissed because the prosecuting attorneys couldn't find two witnesses with collaborating testimonies.

The first — and only — NHL player to die from an injury suffered in an NHL game was Minnesota North Stars forward Bill Masterton, who also scored the first goal in franchise history. On January 13, 1968, Masterton collided with a pair of California Seals defenders while making a blind rush into the offensive zone. He was upended awkwardly and struck his head on the ice. He died in hospital two days later. The Masterton Trophy for perseverance and sportsmanship is awarded in his honor annually by the league.

First NHL player to go from the bar to behind bars

Driven to Distraction

1931

Charles Cahill, who sipped a cup of coffee with the Boston Bruins in 1925–26, went from the NHL to the minors to the big house. In 1931, he was charged with vehicular homicide and spent two years in jail.

Cahill may have been the first, but he wasn't the last. In May of 1984, Boston Bruins forward Craig MacTavish had a few pops too many at the local watering hole and made a deadly decision to drive himself home. Just outside Danvers, Massachusetts, MacTavish's vehicle collided with a car driven by a local resident resulting in the young lady's death. MacTavish was charged with vehicular homicide and sentenced to a lengthy jail sentence. He was also suspended by the NHL and missed the entire 1985–86 season.

As a result of the accident and the negative publicity the case generated in the Boston area, the Bruins had little choice but to hand MacTavish his walking papers. In February of 1985, MacTavish was signed as a free agent by Edmonton and joined the team after being granted parole. After paying his debt to society, MacTavish went on to be known as one the NHL's top defensive forwards and worked diligently and successfully to become one the League's outstanding citizens. He is currently the coach of the Oilers.

First NHL player to be found guilty of manslaughter

Crime and Punishment

1950

Tony Demers, who once played on a line with Elmer Lach and Maurice Richard when he was a member of the Montreal Canadiens, was a spirited sparkplug on the ice, gifted with soft hands and a hard accurate shot. Although he was a speed demon, his size restricted him from maintaining a place on an NHL roster, but he did forge a noteworthy career for himself in the Quebec Senior Hockey League, a loop that many considered to be only a notch below the NHL.

In the final four years of his career in the QSHL, Demers scored 199 goals but his on-ice magic soon became tragic when he was convicted of manslaughter in the death of his girlfriend during the summer of 1950. He was sentenced to 15 years in jail and served eight years in the Bar Hotel before being paroled.

If Demers had been an inmate at Marquette State Prison in Michigan during the 1950s, he may have felt right at home. In 1953, the Marquette prison became the first penitentiary to have an NHL regulation-sized outdoor rink and form its own league. Athletic director and coach Len "Oakie" Brunn was the mastermind behind the idea, and his "varsity" team of inmates actually played "free world" teams. The most famous contest was held in 1955 and it featured the defending Stanley Cup-champion Detroit Red Wings clashing with the convicts in what may be the oddest game ever held that involved an NHL team.

First owner to go from the Stanley Cup penthouse to the jailhouse
Our Pal Hal

1972

ABOVE: Hal and Hope — the bemused grin on Bob Hope's face — which is either pure fright or sheer delight — is all the evidence needed to prove that even the master of the one-liner knew when he was in the company of a real "con" man.

n May of 1972, Harold Ballard, the owner of the Toronto Maple Leafs, was convicted of abusing his shareholders' money to buy motorbikes, rent cars, renovate the cottage and do landscaping at his Toronto home. Ballard stood trial on 49 counts of fraud and theft and was sentenced to three years in Millhaven Prison.

Ballard's partner in crime, Leafs' co-owner Stafford Smythe was also charged with numerous violations and he was certain to suffer the same fate as Ballard. Only days before Smythe's trial was to begin, he died from complications after surgery.

Ballard wasn't the only former NHL owner who was caught with his hands in the till. Former Los Angeles Kings owner Bruce McNall was sentenced to four years in federal prison when he was charged with two counts of bank fraud and one count of wire fraud with another count of wire conspiracy tossed in for good measure. McNall had pilfered 236 million dollars from various sources. McNall served his time in a variety of institutions, all of which had bars, guards and yards — not quite the executive suites McNall was used to when he was embellishing his image and robbing all his buddies blind.

First player to be arrested during a game

Gas Guzzler

1978

BELOW: When Marty McSorley laid the lumber across the head of Vancouver forward Donald Brashear, he became the first NHL player in the modern era to be suspended for life because of a violent on-ice incident.

During a game between the WHA's Birmingham Bulls and Cincinnati Stingers on February 19, 1978, Cincinnati police arrested Bulls' defenseman Frank "Seldom" Beaton and charged him with assault for an altercation at a neighborhood gas station. It seems that gas jockey Gabriel Fieno spilled gasoline on Beaton's Corvette, and refused to clean up his mess. So, Beaton turned the guy black and blue and went off to the rink, where six of Cincy's finest found him and took him downtown.

Another NHL player who frequently found himself on the wrong arm of the law in often hilarious circumstances was Link Gaetz, a bruising defenseman who tore up the NHL in the early 1990s. Unfortunately for Gaetz, the tearing up he did occurred off the ice and it often landed him in the cooler. His misconduct was mostly caused by alcohol and involved such childish pranks as stealing the odd TV, causing the odd disturbance and tossing the odd TV through the nearest hotel window.

Link never lost his sense of humor, though. In 1999, Gaetz was arraigned on a charge of public intoxication after a drunken rampage in Texas. When he was brought before Judge Barbara Hale and informed that his bond would be set at $10,000, Gaetz retorted, "Ah, make it $100,000."

"So I did," Judge Hale recalled as she watched the bailiff slap the cuffs on Gaetz and lead him off to his new home in the Huntsville city jail.

Gaetz has since cleaned up his act and returned to what he does best, playing diligent and gritty defense for Sagenay Paramedic of the Quebec Semi-Professional Hockey League.

Acknowledgments

Kelly Anderson/HHOF: p 5

Roy Antal/HHOF: p 55 (top)

Babineau/HHOF: pp 44 (top), 55 (bottom right), 111, 119

Paul Bereswill: pp 2, 12 (bottom), 16, 17, 18, 22 (top), 33 (right), 38, 39, 44 (bottom), 46, 67 (bottom), 77, 84, 85, 93, 94 (left), 115 (right), 130 (both), 137 (bottom), 147 (left), 153

Bettmann/Corbis: pp 6 (top right), 43 (bottom left and right), 45, 103 (top), 133 (top), 134 (top), 146 (right)

Anthony Biegun/HHOF: p 69

Jim Callaway/NCAA Photos: p 80

Tom Dahlin/HHOF: p 107

DiMaggio/HHOF: p 60 (right)

Ernie Fitzsimmons Collection: pp 6 (left and bottom), 7 (both), 15 (right), 20 (right), 34, 35 (top), 37, 47 (bottom right), 48 (right), 58 (top), 59 (top), 91 (left), 92, 97 (left), 101, 105 (both), 117 (top), 124 (top), 128, 131, 150, 151 (top left), 154

Ernie Fitzsimmons/HHOF: 33 (left), 81, 129 (top)

Bob Fondriest/HHOF: p 70

Graphic Artists/HHOF: pp 21 (top), 22 (bottom), 26, 27, 30 (middle), 62 (bottom), 75 (right), 78 (both), 108 (right), 113 (bottom), 122, 124 (bottom), 125 (bottom), 140 (bottom), 151 (bottom), 152

Lisa Harmatuk/HHOF: p 136

Hockey Hall of Fame Archives: pp 13 (bottom), 15 (left), 21 (bottom), 24 (both), 29 (both), 35, 36 (top), 40 (both), 42, 43 (top), 47 (bottom left), 58 (bottom), 59 (bottom left and right), 60 (left), 64, 65 (both), 68 (top), 72 (top), 76 (both), 89, 90, 94 (right), 95, 96, 97 (right), 100 (right), 102, 104 (both), 110 (bottom), 112, 116 (left), 117 (bottom), 120, 121, 123, 126, 134 (bottom), 137 (top), 138 (top), 139, 141, 144, 146 (left), 147 (right)

Hulton-Deutsch Collection/Corbis: p 52
Doug MacLellan/HHOF: pp 11 (top), 20 (left), 48 (left), 86, 98 (left), 115 (left), 133 (bottom), 135, 142

Matthew Manor/HHOF: p 10 (bottom)

Mecca/HHOF: pp 30 (left and right), 32, 125 (top), 129 (bottom), 149

Miles Nadal/HHOF: p 143 (bottom)

Minnesota Historical Society/Corbis: p 53

O-Pee-Chee/HHOF: pp 99 (left), 140 (top)

Ottawa Citizen/HHOF: p 143 (top)

Steve Ozimec/HHOF: p 113 (top)

London Life — Portnoy/HHOF: pp 10 (top right), 19, 23 (right), 75 (left), 83, 87, 99 (right), 110 (top), 114

Frank Prazak/HHOF: pp 28 (left), 36 (bottom), 57, 62 (top)

Princeton Univeristy Library: p 88

Reuters NewMedia Inc./Corbis: pp 103 (bottom), 156

James Rice/HHOF: p 74

Rykoff Collection/Corbis: p 63

Dave Sandford/HHOF: pp 4, 8, 14 (bottom), 25 (top), 49 (both), 50, 54, 55 (bottom left), 56, 67 (top), 68 (bottom), 71, 72 (bottom), 73 (both), 118, 138 (bottom), 151 (top left)

Dave Sandford/IIHF: pp 12 (top), 41 (both), 47 (top)

Larry Sexton/HHOF: p 106

Imperial Oil — Turofsky/HHOF: pp 9, 10 (top left), 11 (bottom), 13 (top), 14 (top), 23 (left), 25 (bottom), 31, 51, 66 (both), 79, 82, 91 (right), 98 (left), 108 (left), 109, 116 (right), 127, 132 (both), 145, 148, 155

Underwood & Underwood/Corbis: p 61